Contents

Advaita on Zen
Comments on Huang Po

The Chün Chou Record of Huang Po

Preface

The Chün Chou Record is a short diary written by P'ei Hsiu detailing the talks he heard of the great Zen Master Hsi Yün, sometime around 850CE in the city of Chün Chou, China. Hsi Yün lived as a hermit for many years on Mount Huang Po, and became known posthumously by that name alone. He is regarded as one of the great masters of the southern branch of the Zen sect of Buddhism, which taught the doctrine of non-duality, or 'sudden enlightenment'.

Just as English is recognisably the same language whether spoken in America, England, or India, the various teachings of non-duality, whether from Lao Tzu, Bankei, or Ashtavakra, all point to the same non-conceptual Truth. Consider the following, "The existence of things as separate entities or not as separate entities are both dualistic concepts… a man drinking water knows well enough if it is cold or warm." This quotation of Huang Po (Wan Chi Record, 50) could easily have been written by Ramesh S. Balsekar, the modern Indian Advaita Master. In the following pages, Ramesh brings home this point in his commentaries on the Chün Chou Record. He begins each section by paraphrasing the original wording of Huang Po's talks, and then goes on to elucidate its meaning in the conceptual framework of Advaita Vedanta.

A few reference points to differences in the wording of some key concepts may be helpful: Zen uses the word 'Mind' to refer to what Advaita calls either 'Consciousness'

or 'Impersonal Awareness', and uses 'mind' for what Advaita would call the personal consciousness, or ego (which in the ordinary person is based on the sense of personal doership and the thinking mind). Where Huang Po says, "When body and mind achieve spontaneity, the Way is reached, and Mind is understood"(chpt. 29), Advaita might say, "In the absence of the sense of personal doership, all actions are seen to be spontaneously arising appearances in Consciousness, Awareness-in-motion, which is all there is." And, when Huang Po uses the word 'Buddha', as in, "The Ever-Existent Buddha is not a Buddha of form or attachment" (chpt. 2), he is not referring to a man who lived in India 2500 years ago. Similarly, Ramesh does not mean a very old man with a white beard passing judgement on sinners when he uses the word 'God'. They are both referring to the Source – Eternity – pure Subjectivity devoid of any objectivity, which is what we truly Are.

INTRODUCTION
BY RAMESH BALSEKAR

In the teachings of the Zen Masters can surely be seen the brilliant exposition of some valid inner realisation of the basic Truth, not unlike the exposition of the same basic Truth in Advaita, by masters like Adi Shankaracharya and the sage Jnaneshwar. Indeed, there is the theory that Bodhidharma arrived in China bringing with him a doctrine of great antiquity from India.

Huang Po is regarded by many as the founder of the great Lin Chi (Rinzai) Sect which still continues in China and flourishes widely in Japan. Huang Po is generally known in Japan as Obaku.

Zen followers are not content to pursue Enlightenment through eons of varied rebirths, inevitably burdened with pain and ignorance, approaching with infinite slowness the supreme experience which Christian mystics have described as 'union with the Godhead'. They believe in the possibility of the happening of full Enlightenment through going beyond conceptual thinking and grasping the Intuitive Understanding.

This book has been broadly based on *The Zen Teaching of Huang Po,* translated by John Blofeld in 1958.

1. The Master said, "All sentient beings, including the Buddhas, are in reality nothing but the One Mind: It is all that exists. This Mind is without beginning and is indestructible. It has neither form nor colour, and transcends all attributes and comparisons. It is That which exists before you, the boundless void that cannot be measured; start thinking about it and you fall into error.

The sentient beings, attached to form, seek externally for Buddhahood, and are not aware that whatever they do for a full eon, they will be frustrated. They do not understand that if only they stop their conceptualising and worrying, they will realise that the One Mind is the Buddha and the Buddha is all living beings. This One Mind is not greater in the Buddha and smaller in the ordinary man."

According to Advaita:

a) I dream the universe, and all that is dreamt is 'I' – I who am but not as a 'me'; you perceive the universe, but you ARE only as 'I' and not as any 'you'.

b) I alone can look, but I do not see what is seen by a 'me'; I alone can speak, but I do not say what is said by a 'me'; I alone function, but I do not do what is done by a 'me'. *I AM, but there is no 'me' or 'you' or 'him' or 'her'.*

c) I am the seeing of all that is seen; the hearing of all that is heard; the knowing of all that is known or can be known; I am the Awareness of all that is aware, the conceiving of all that can be conceived and, therefore, I cannot be conceived.

'I' can only be 'conceived' as AWARENESS, unaware of being aware.

2. You are the Buddha-Mind, fundamentally complete in all respects; it is futile to supplement that perfection by any meaningless practices like performing the six paramitas (charity, morality, patience under affliction, zealous application, right control of mind, and the application of the highest wisdom), and many similar practices, or gaining merits as countless as the sands of the Ganga. You may perform them whenever you like performing them, but not under compulsion. Otherwise, your way of thinking is not compatible with the Way. To make use of your mind and think conceptually is to attach yourselves to the form and miss the substance. The ever-present Buddha is not a Buddha of form. Just awake to the One Mind, and there is nothing whatsoever to be attained.

The Buddha and all sentient beings are the One Mind and nothing else.

According to Advaita, what is at the root of bondage and unhappiness is the sense of personal doership, the notion of volition. The entire mechanism of daily living is based on the notion that volition is behind every act of the human being and that, therefore, he is 'responsible' for those acts. The fact of the matter, however, is that human beings do not 'act' but 'react' to an outside stimulus. Most of the time living, for most people, is conditioned by a series of reflexes based essentially on instinct, habit and even propaganda. The scope of deliberate, considered action is in actual life extremely limited, and yet almost every person firmly believes that he is the doer, and it is for this reason that the sage Ashtavakra refers to this notion of individual volition as the bite of the deadly serpent, the ego.

The only practice which can free man from the poison of personal doership is the abandonment of the identification with a particular object as a separate entity with doership. Human beings may think that they live their lives, but in fact their lives are being lived as part of the total functioning of this entire manifestation. All events together constitute the functioning of the manifestation according to the inexorable chain of causation. It would be incredible to imagine that such functioning of Totality could leave any scope for individual volition except, of course, as part of that very functioning.

The only remedy for the snakebite of doership is the 'faith' that the human being exists not as an individual body-mind entity – a mere object – but as Noumenon*, the One Subject. Such faith brings about the sudden and spontaneous understanding that 'I' am the One Subject and the entire manifestation is My objective expression. 'I Am' the Universal Consciousness within which has spontaneously arisen the totality of the phenomenal manifestation, the functioning of which is what we call our daily living.

---

* Noumenon: A word widely used by the great philosopher Immanuel Kant to show the distinction between the invisible world of Reality (Noumenon) and the apparent world of sensible 'phenomena'.

3. The sun shines throughout the four corners of the world and illuminates the whole earth but the void does not gain in brilliance, nor does the void darken when the sun sets. The phenomena of light and dark are the basic duality of the manifestation, but the nature of the void remains unchanged.

If you look upon sentient beings as a foul, dark or a mortal-seeming appearance while you look upon the Buddha as a pure, bright, Enlightened being, such conceptual thinking, resulting from attachment to form, will keep you away from the Supreme Understanding. If you are not awake to the fact that there is only the One Mind and not a particle of anything else to get hold of, you will overlay Mind with more and more conceptual thinking which will make you seek the Buddha outside of yourself, and you will remain attached to forms, pious practices and similar things which will keep you away from the Supreme Understanding.

Advaita tells us that sudden enlightenment comes about only through an understanding which needs no effort of any kind. The basis of sudden enlightenment is the deep understanding that there cannot exist any individual as such, because all there is, is Consciousness, in which appears the totality of the manifestation, including the individual human beings.

Just as sunlight makes objects in a room perceivable but is not concerned with what happens to the objects, it is in Consciousness that all phenomenal objects appear, and all such objects are perceived and cognised by Consciousness through the sentient objects, but Consciousness is not involved in what happens to the objects.

The Witness cannot be the doer, and you are not a phenomenal object but Consciousness which merely witnesses the operations in the manifest world. With this understanding, detachment from the wrong identification with the body as an individual doer of deeds can take place. The state of being disidentified from the body as the individual doer of deeds is the state of witnessing. And this state of detached witnessing is indeed the state of liberation from the bondage of doership.

What is needed is to remain relaxed in and as Consciousness. No rigorous practices and disciplines are needed. All that is needed for enlightenment *to occur* is a clear understanding of a dimension that is quite different from intellectual comprehension. Belief is different from faith. Intellectual comprehension brings about a belief in what is comprehended but an intuitive apprehension is based on faith. Belief is based on argumentation, logic, effort and conflict; intuitive apprehension – faith or apperception* – is based on a certain inescapable inevitability, a relaxed and total acceptance of 'what-is', that opens the 'eye of the heart' to apperceive the Truth.

---

* Apperception: Mind's perception of itself. (Concise Oxford Dictionary)

A term that was coined by Leibniz in his New Essays (1696), widely used by Immanuel Kant and Terence Gray (Wei Wu Wei).

4. It is much better to revere the one who has had the Ultimate Understanding than to make offerings to all the Buddhas of the universe, because the Enlightened one has been rid of all conceptualisation.

The Absolute is neither subjective nor objective, has no particular location, is formless and, therefore, cannot vanish. What may be considered as the substance of the Absolute is inwardly motionless and outwardly like the void, without either obstructions or boundaries. Those who seek the goal through cognition, the many, hasten toward the Absolute, but dare not enter it for fear of being hurtled down the void, with nothing to hold on to. So they go up to the brink and retreat with their conceptualising.

Few are those who receive intuitive knowledge of the Way.

According to Advaita, it is only when the sense of Presence – I AM – arises on the original state of Unicity that Consciousness concurrently comes into movement and brings forth upon Itself the totality of manifestation. The movement of Consciousness also simultaneously brings about the concepts of knowledge (I AM, the sense of *impersonal* Presence) and ignorance (when the impersonal Presence becomes identified with each sentient being as a separate, volitional entity).

The unicity of the potential plenum – the I-Subject – gets dichotomised in the process of manifestation as subject and object – the 'me' and the 'other' – each object considering itself as the pseudo-subject-observer *vis-à-vis* all other observed objects. This itself is the conceptual bondage of the individual, and liberation consists in the realisation that our true nature has always been the Impersonal Consciousness and not the psychosomatic apparatus with which Consciousness has identified Itself (so that the functioning of manifestation, as daily living, could take place through interhuman relationships).

When such a realisation happens – the metanoesis or *para-vritti* – the pseudo-subject ceases to be an object and becomes void by the superimposition of the opposites (subject-object), and through this void or nothingness, returns to the original I-Subject, the potential plenum. This total potentiality – the I-Subject – cannot offer Itself for comprehension because then it would be an object. The eye can see everything else, but the eye cannot see itself.

5. 'Manjushri' means the fundamental law of the Real and unbounded Void, 'Samantabhadra' means the inexhaustible activities beyond the sphere of form; 'Avalokiteshwara' represents boundless compassion, 'Mahasthama' the great wisdom, and 'Vimalakirti' the spotless name referring to the real nature of things.

There are the students of the Way who are not aware that all the qualities typified by the Bodhisattvas are inherent in human beings, and are not to be separated from the One Mind. They are not aware of this important fact and are either attached to appearances or seek for something objective outside their own minds, and have thus turned their backs on the Way.

As the Buddha has put it:

"If all the Buddhas and Bodhisattvas, with Indra and all the gods, walk across them, the sands of the Ganga do not rejoice; and if oxen, sheep, reptiles and insects tread upon them, the sands are not angered. For jewels and perfumes they have no longing, and for the stinking filth of manure and urine they have no loathing."

The Advaitic concept of *Sat-Chit-Ananda* is an attempt to describe the indescribable. Presence cannot produce presence; manifestation cannot produce manifestation. Phenomena that can be sensorially perceived can be produced (can become present) only from the potential (absence) that is the Noumenon. But, the absence is not an absent 'thing' that is not perceivable sensorially, because in that sense it would be 'not present'. The Noumenon, the Absolute Absence, is the source of all objectivity, which Advaita has called *Sat-Chit-Ananda* (existence-consciousness-peace) because people have, in the phenomenal sense, always felt the need of a positive approach to better comprehend the point.

The term 'noumenon' may be used either as the counterpart of the term 'phenomenon', or more accurately, to indicate the non-objective source of all cognition. The actual counterpart of 'phenomenon' can only be 'non-phenomenon'; the mutual negation of *both*, the absence of 'non-phenomenon', would be Noumenon.

Advaita has called Noumenon *Sat-Chit-Ananda* as a positive practical approach. Unfortunately, *Ananda* has usually been translated as 'bliss', but the more accurate term would be 'peace'. But, fundamentally, it must be clearly understood that Noumenon means the absence of both phenomena and non-phenomena.

In fact, the three attributes are not to be understood literally or separately. It is really necessary to apperceive the understanding behind the words. The totality of the three words must be understood as PEACE. 'Peace' does not mean positive joy or pleasure but the absolute abolition of suffering in both the positive and the negative sense. 'PEACE' is supposed to indicate both the absence of the presence of suffering and the absence of the absence of suffering: a norm of equilibrium that cannot be experienced relatively.

Being unmanifest, the Absolute Absence knows neither intellectuality nor affectivity, both being concerned with phenomenal presence. This absence, this void, known as *Sat-Chit-Ananda,* would need some explanation:

Brightness, hardness and the gold itself all together mean 'gold'.

Whiteness, softness and fragrance together combine to make camphor. Just as the whiteness and the softness of camphor merge into the pervading fragrance, similarly, existence and Consciousness merge in the supreme, intense feeling of PEACE.

6. The One Mind is not the mind of conceptual thinking and is totally detached from form. It is for this reason that the Buddhas and sentient beings are not fundamentally different. If you could rid yourself of conceptual thinking, you would not need anything more. If, however, you are not able to rid yourself instantly of your conceptual thinking, you will never accomplish anything even if you strive for eon after eon; enmeshed in the usual practices of the Three Vehicles, you will never be able to attain Enlightenment.

There are those who, upon hearing the teaching, have been able to rid themselves of conceptual thinking in a flash; there are others who are able to do this after following through the Ten Beliefs, the Ten Stages, the Ten Activities, and the Ten Bestowals of Merit; yet others are able to achieve it after passing through the Ten Stages of a Bodhisattva's Progress. (The conceptualised *form* of a Buddha, to whom the unenlightened pray, is truly unreal inasmuch as he is regarded as an entity and, as such, is quite apart from the One Mind.)

Whether the transcendence of conceptual thinking happens by a longer or a shorter way, the result is a state of 'BEING' – there is no question of any pious practising and no action of realising.

The Ten Stages of a Bodhisattva's Progress merely entails eons of unnecessary suffering and toil.

In the Advaita tradition, the sage Ashtavakra tells his royal disciple:

"If you detach yourself from the identification with the ego as an individual doer, and remain relaxed in and as Impersonal Consciousness, you will, this very moment, be happy, at peace and free from bondage."

This is the very core of the teaching, and can stun the seeker into a spiritual shock. The seeker immersed in a host of practices and disciplines expects to have to do hard work for a long time to 'achieve' enlightenment.

The understanding which leads to sudden enlightenment comes about merely through a very, very deep apperception, much deeper than an intellectual acceptance, which needs no effort of any kind. The basis of this very important concept is:

a) 'You' are not the body-mind organism that is composed of the five elements; you are that Consciousness which has provided that inert body with the sentience that evokes the senses to function in relation to their objects. It is sentience which makes the psychosomatic apparatus work as a unit.

b) 'You' are not the physical organism but Consciousness which works not as some entity in charge of the operations but merely as the Witness of the operations.

c) The Witness cannot be the doer of any action. With this understanding, you can detach yourself from the wrong identification with the body, and then you will naturally assume your true position as the Witness of whatever happens through any body-mind organism as the functioning of Consciousness, and not the doing by any individual entity.

d) Just as sunlight makes objects in a room perceivable but is not concerned with what happens to the objects themselves, it is in Consciousness that all phenomenal objects appear, and such objects are perceived and cognised by Consciousness through the sentient beings. But, Consciousness is not involved in what happens to the phenomenal objects, including human beings.

e) The state of being disidentified with the body, as the doer of any deed, is the state of witnessing. And that, indeed, is the state of liberation which is sudden and immediate.

7. Building up the good and leaving off the evil both involve attachment to form. Those who do evil are supposed to undergo various incarnations unnecessarily, while those who, being attached to form, do good, subject themselves to trials and tribulations equally, all to no purpose. The goal, in either case, is to achieve Self-realisation by grasping the fundamental Dharma. This Dharma and Mind are not different. Mind in itself, is not mind; and yet it is not no-mind either, because no-mind implies something that exists. In other words, Mind is an arbitrary term for something that simply cannot be adequately expressed in words.

What is really needed is a mere silent, deep understanding *without words*, without any thinking and conceptualising. In other words, what is needed is the cutting off of words and the elimination of the movements of mind.

The Mind is the pure Buddha-Source inherent in sentient beings, both human beings and all wriggling beings. All the Buddhas and the Bodhisattvas are of this One Substance and, in this sense, there is no difference between them. Differences arise only from unnecessary conceptualising and wrong-thinking that can only lead to all kinds of unnecessary karma.

Advaita clearly acknowledges the value of the 'word'. It is because of the word that sound assumes the dignity of meaning. It can indicate the nature of what is sensorially not perceptible and is, therefore, a mirror to the Unmanifest. The usual mirror enables only the one who has eyesight to see the reflection of his face, but the word has the power to enable even one without eyesight to see his real Self.

The word is born in the unique family of the Unmanifest, and it is the word that has given the name *ambar* to the sky, or to space. It is like the sun which brings into existence what otherwise would have remained unseen. The word

'Unmanifest' has been used with different interpretations in the traditional Advaita texts. Whether in the *Brahma Sutra* or the *Bhagavad Gita* the common factor is, of course, that the *word denotes something beyond sensorial perception.*

The Unmanifest becomes manifest only with the arising of Consciousness on the Absolute – 'I AM'. But the fact remains that what is manifest does not have any independent existence. The phenomenal objects are merely reflections or illusions which owe such existence to *Maya* – thought, conceptualisation, or the 'word'.

The Sanskrit word *ambar* means the 'word'; the word holds space and, therefore, space (the sky) is also called *ambar*. It is only through conceptualisation that the medium of space has been created within which phenomenal objects can be perceived; and thus the concept of space and along with it the conceptual universe are 'created' as appearances in Consciousness. It is the word that has created both the concepts of the Absolute-Unmanifest and the relative-manifest.

The word, like the proverbial 'flower in the sky', is non-existent, but it produces fruit in the form of the manifested universe; there is nothing in the world that can be called 'immeasurable' when it can be measured by the word. Other than the Absolute which is pure Subjectivity, nothing else can really be said to exist. All things owe their existence to the word; a word is itself merely a concept but it is instrumental in creating all the conditioning that makes the individual accept something non-existent as existent.

So long as there is no realisation of the non-existence of the word, the individual continues to accept the conditioning conveyed by the word and also continues, as an object, to suffer all the experiences associated with living in this conceptual world.

It is the word which conveys to the world the dos and the don'ts which every religion seems to insist on. It is also the word that brings into existence the concepts of bondage and liberation.

There have been so many reformers, religious heads, prophets and philosophers, each with his own code of dos and don'ts for attaining self-transcendence, but nothing has changed in the world. People have been branded as heretics and unbelievers, and whipped and tortured, ironically not in anger but in sorrow, "for the good of their immortal souls!" Obviously, it is the word which has goaded people to such excesses, not only to maim and kill others, but also to suffer themselves and perish in their religious zeal.

Then there are the words 'bondage' and 'liberation'. It is the word which gives the message that one should treat the 'other' as oneself, and thereby at once creates bondage by announcing that there is the 'other'. In reality there is neither the 'one' nor the 'other'. This conditioning gets stronger and stronger as the word piles on more verbiage. The fact of the matter is that in the absence of consciousness, in deep sleep for example, Consciousness is subjective, impersonal. Each one of us is, in reality, 'I', the only Subject, without any object at all. As Subject, one just IS, here and now.

In the process of manifestation, the Impersonal Consciousness becomes identified with each phenomenal entity, which thereafter regards itself as the subject of all other objects. The ego is the illusory effect of such identification, necessary for the functioning of the manifestation as daily living, based on interpersonal relationships.

8. It is the truth that the original Buddha-Nature is totally devoid of any atom of objectivity. It is the void of purity itself, silent, omnipresent, *glorious mysterious joyful peace.* Nothing else. One must awaken oneself, suddenly and totally. Whatever is, is utterly complete, in its total fullness; nothing else exists.

Whether you realise it by all the various tedious stages, with eons of work and achievement, or you attain to full realisation in a flash and realise that these eons of hard work were no better than unreal actions performed in a dream, you will only be realising the Buddha-Nature which was never away from you. That is why the Tathagata is reported to have said, "I truly attained nothing from complete, unexcelled Enlightenment. Had there been anything attained, Dipamkara Buddha would not have made the prophecy concerning me."

This quotation refers to the *Diamond Sutra*, in which Dipamkara Buddha, during a former life of Gautama Buddha, prophesised that he would one day attain to Buddhahood. "Huang Po means that the prophesy would not have been made if Dipamkara Buddha had supposed that Gautama Buddha's enlightenment would lead to the actual attainment of something he had not already *been* from the very first; for then Enlightenment would not have led to Buddhahood, which implies a voidness of all distinctions such as attainer, attained, non-attainer, and non-attained."*

The Tathagata is also supposed to have said, "This Dharma is absolutely without distinctions, neither high nor low, and its name is Bodhi." As Pure Mind, it is the primal Source of everything, without the slightest distinction of selfness or otherness, whether appearing as sentient beings or Buddhas, as the rivers and mountains of the world, whether with form or without form.

* From Blofeld's footnotes to the original text.

Advaita points out very clearly that what is necessary for the metanoesis – transformation or *para-vritti* – to occur is the apprehension by the apparent seeker of his own utter non-existence as an autonomous entity. It is only such apprehension which can lead to a clean sundering of the abominable chain of continuous conceptualising in temporal phenomenality. This apprehension can reveal the noumenal Immensity, the Infinite Intemporality – that we really are. This is beyond the word to accomplish because the word is itself the product of phenomenal duality and thus inevitably restricted by the parameters of the phenomenal framework. Apperception must happen before the apparent seeker can be annihilated.

A notion-thought-word about an object that arises in the mind is evoked or produced by an outside stimulus and receives its 'substance' from memory. This is how the thought, the word, is born. Thus, the 'reality' of any object – as near as a chair or as distant as a star – is nothing but an image in the mind, and the mind is nothing but the content of Consciousness. In other words, an object is perceived because of an impression in the mind which gathers its substance by incredibly rapid repetitions of that impression. In scientific terms, each repetition is a 'separate quantum', and a series of such quanta constitutes what we know as 'time'.

What we imagine as the 'reality' of an object is nothing but a continuous series of impressions following one another at incredible speed. The basis of both the manifestation of objects as well as the time or duration in which it occurs is Consciousness.

All so-called 'reality' is, therefore, conceptual (the thought, the word) and phenomenal; and it is only by the negation of this phenomenal conceptualisation (the word sacrificing itself) that noumenality – the true Reality that we are – can be apperceived. All that is positive and objective is the handiwork of the word/thought. It is only with the negating of conceptualising that this handiwork can be erased, leaving only a phenomenal emptiness or void, which represents Absolute Noumenal Presence. In this state the thought process has ended, resulting in the inconceivable, where the thought/word is totally and indubitably barred.

It is important to realise that all that is necessary is to get rid of conceptualising, not ignorance as such but the concept of ignorance itself. For the Truth to reveal itself – sudden awakening – all that is necessary is the negation of the mistaken identification as a separate entity with autonomy and volition. There is nothing to be 'achieved' because any acquisition can only be one of the pair of interrelated opposites.

The transcending of conceptualising cannot happen by suppressing concepts, but with the understanding that there is nothing to be achieved; and this means abstaining from pursuing desires. Being free from purposeful intention means being free from conceptualising; without volition, our acts become spontaneous and, therefore, free from guilt and shame. Freedom or abstention from volitional action includes both volitional action and volitional non-action. Such absence of positive as well as negative volitional or conceptional activity keeps the mind in a state of vacancy, fasting or equilibrium and, therefore, open to the sudden, spontaneous apperception that leads to metanoesis – *para-vritti* – liberation from conceptual bondage.

9. The people of the world regard only that as mind which sees, hears, feels and knows, and are not awake to the fact that it is the Pure Mind, the Source, that shines forever on everything with the brilliance of its own perfection. They do not perceive the spiritual brilliance of the Source-Substance because they are too blinded by what they consider their own sight, hearing, feeling and knowing.

If only they would give up all conceptual thinking, they would realise in a flash that it is that Source-Substance which manifests itself like the sun ascending through the void and illuminating the whole universe without any hindrance or boundaries.

If you continue to seek to progress through your own seeing, hearing, feeling and knowing, you will find your way to Mind cut off and you will be lost when you are deprived of your perceptions. It is necessary to realise that these perceptions happen only through the Pure Mind, though it neither forms part of them, nor is separate from them. You should not start *reasoning* from those perceptions, nor let them give rise to conceptualising and objectivising.

Above, below, and around you, all exists spontaneously. Neither keep your perceptions nor abandon them, nor dwell in them, nor cling to them. There is nowhere that is outside the Buddha-Mind.

There is not a single moment when one is not conscious of being present for the simple reason that what we are in our conscious state cannot be anything other than Consciousness. Our bondage is 'ignorance', and the fact of the matter is that we are conscious of our ignorance, and ignorance, as such, cannot have an independent existence or nature of its own apart from knowledge i.e. consciousness of being present.

According to Advaita, the basic theme of Unicity (non-duality), is that Awareness resides in the Absolute state (*avyakta*): Consciousness in repose, not conscious of Itself. It pervades the inner Self (*vyakta*), while the outer self or the individual (*vyakti*) is that state of being where one is conscious but not 'Aware'. In other words, the outer self (*vyakti*) is delineated by the physical body, the inner Self (*vyakta*) by Consciousness, and it is only in pure Awareness that the Absolute (*avyakta*) prevails.

In other words, when Awareness is in contact with an object, a physical form, witnessing comes into operation: the object is sensorially perceived but not compared and judged. When the individual is identified as a separate entity with volition, the contact with an object is no longer mere witnessing but becomes the individual entity observing together with comparing and judging. But the very important fact is that *there is only one state*. When corrupted and tainted by personal doership, the state is called the ego, the individual entity; when merely tinted by a sense of impersonal Presence, of animated Consciousness, it becomes the witnessing; when it remains in its pristine purity, untainted and untinted, in primal repose, it is the Absolute.

With the arising of Consciousness in that primal state of pure Awareness, when Consciousness was not conscious of Itself, the first thought arose: I AM, the direct and immediate *impersonal* thought, what the Chinese sage Shou Hui termed 'absolute thought'.

In the witnessing state, daily living becomes merely witnessing of events that take place in this living dream. Such living, in the man of understanding, is outwardly like that of any other individual, but inwardly it is without any identification of any event with any individual, volitional separate entity. Any thought through such a separate, volitional entity objectifies everything all the time, because that is its nature and function in what we know as daily living. It is such objectivisation, through volition and the pursuit of desire, that is the cause of the conceptual bondage with its need for liberation for this conceptual entity, the ego.

10. What happens when people hear it said that the Buddhas transmit the 'Doctrine of the Mind', is they mistakenly believe that it is something to be achieved through the mind, through thinking and conceptualising, not knowing that the Mind and the object of their search are the same.

The fundamental Dharma is the sudden elimination of conceptualising and objectivising, and for this purpose the mind cannot be used to seek the Pure Mind. It is like a man looking for his spectacles when he has pushed them back on his forehead. All that anyone can do is merely point out to him that he had never lost his spectacles and there was no question of 'finding' his spectacles. It is precisely because of this mistake that people keep indulging in various achievements and hard practices, expecting to attain Self-realisation through such graduated practices.

The various methods that are usually recommended cannot be compared to the sudden elimination of conceptual thinking by the *total* understanding that there simply can be nothing at all which has absolute existence – nothing on which to lay hold, nothing on which to rely, nothing in which to abide, nothing subjective or objective. It is for this reason that the Buddha is supposed to have said, "I truly attained nothing from complete, unexcelled Enlightenment." Actually it was indeed because he feared that the truth was too simple for people to accept easily, that he must have felt compelled to draw upon what is seen with the five sorts of vision and to speak with the five kinds of speech.

What is repeated very often in Advaita is the fact that there is no basic difference between the manifest (*vyakta*) and the Unmanifest (*avyakta*), just as there is no essential difference between light and daylight. The universe is full of light, but that light cannot be seen unless it is reflected against a surface as daylight; what the daylight reveals is the individual entity (*vyakti*). The individual entity is always the object (although the sense of doership makes him think he is the subject and the other is the object). The individual is always the object while Consciousness (as the witnessing) is the Subject.

The world, though it appears 'real', is merely an appearance within Consciousness and so the world can be said *to 'appear' but not to 'be'*. The appearance that is present – the presence of phenomenon – can only happen in the absence of the noumenon. The world, and the phenomena therein, are thus the totality of the known in the immensity of the unknown potential. In Consciousness the world and the phenomena appear and disappear, but all there IS is the impersonal 'I'. Before all beginnings and after all endings, 'I'am the eternal Witness: 'me', 'you', 'he' and 'she' are mere appearances in 'I', or Consciousness.

In other words, anything sensorially perceived is in reality not something that has actually happened as an external event or experience, but is only something that has taken place as a movement in Consciousness. What is more important is the fact that not only is everything not experienced by a 'you', but that 'you' as a separate entity just do not exist. When a flag flutters in the breeze, it is neither the flag nor the breeze that is of any significance, because both the flag and the wind are the contents of the Consciousness in which the event takes place.

Ignorance, as such, does not exist. An illusion or hallucination is only a phenomenon, a happening; in reality there is no such thing because before, during and after the realisation that it was an illusion, nothing like it ever existed. Similarly, there is no such thing as a dream except as a phenomenon, as a happening, an apparent function of dream-ING; the objects perceived by the senses therein are not independent entities at all. When the supposed dreamer wakes up from sleep, the dream-ING ends, and the hopes and fears of any of the dreamed characters are totally non-existent. So also, in this living dream of life, the awakened sage realises that all the characters, including himself, are nothing but phenomenal objects of the dreamer-Source in the objectivisation in Consciousness that this 'daily living' is.

Nothing has actually happened: only waves have appeared on the expanse of water. Nonetheless, in the process of understanding, it is necessary to be clear about the difference, notional though it be, between the Awareness of the Absolute Noumenon and the Consciousness in which the phenomenal manifestation occurs. Manifestation is the reflection of the Absolute, but the reflection of the sun in the dewdrop is not the sun. In deep sleep, in the absence of objectivisation, there is no apparent universe, but we ARE, because on awakening, we know that we were sleeping. In other words, what-we-ARE and the apparent universe are dual in presence (when Consciousness is present, as in the waking state) and non-dual in absence, separate in conceptualisation but inseparable when unconceived.

It is conceptually impossible to comprehend what-we-ARE because mind cannot transcend itself to become Mind. All that we can dialectically conclude is that for anything to be comprehended, there must necessarily be a comprehender. It is this comprehender, who considers himself to be in bondage and seeks liberation, who is caught in a perpetual regression. In the duality of the split-mind (subject-object), in which the comprehending subject in turn becomes the object of another comprehender, the 'who' cannot be eliminated. The cruel joke is that the conceiver-ego, comprehending that the ego must disappear, cannot even think that 'he' is not, because by the very act of saying so he admits that he is very much there.

The fact of the matter is that, unfortunately, in the study of Advaita, too much importance has been given to the fact that there is, in reality, no individual entity, that the ego does not exist. The fact of the matter is that the ego can never be unaware of the fact that he exists as an individual entity, who has to live his life in the circumstances in which he has been placed, and face the pains, trials and tribulations of life. He, therefore, finds it extraordinarily difficult to accept that the ego does not exist.

Not enough importance has been given to the very important fact that the bondage that the ego feels is based on the sense of volition and doership that the ego believes in. As the sage Ashtavakra tells his royal disciple, King Janaka, "You have been bitten by the deadly black serpent of the ego and you therefore consider yourself the doer. Drink the nectar of the faith that you are not the doer of any deed, and be happy."

And yet it is firmly believed by the human being that he is the doer of his actions. As long as this condition remains, so long as there is identification with a phenomenal object as an individual autonomous doer, so long will the bondage continue. Human beings may think that they 'live' their lives, but in fact lives are being lived as part of the total functioning of the entire phenomenal manifestation. All events together constitute the functioning of the manifestation according to the inexorable chain of causation, which cannot leave any room for individual volition. Individual volition, every individual doing whatever he thinks he should do in any given situation, does exist as a part of the mechanism of daily living, but no one ever has any control over the results of 'his actions'.

It is for this reason that the sage Ashtavakra refers to 'faith' as the only remedy for the snakebite of doership – the faith that the human being exists not as an individual entity but as a phenomenal object, through which the Noumenon acts as the One Subject. Such faith brings about the spontaneous and sudden understanding that 'I', the Noumenon, is the only Subject and the phenomenal manifestation is the objective expression of the One Subject – 'I'. 'I' am the impersonal, Universal Consciousness within which has spontaneously arisen the totality of the phenomenal manifestation.

11. Students of the Way must be able to accept totally that the body is neither 'self' nor an individual entity, that the four elements comprising the body cannot constitute the 'self', and that the 'self' is not an individual entity. Moreover, the five aggregates composing the 'mind' – not 'Mind' – do not constitute either the 'self' or an entity. Therefore, it must be accepted that the so-called individual mind is neither 'self' nor an entity.

The five sense organs and the brain, with the six types of perception, and the six kinds of objects of perception, constituting the sensory world, similarly do not constitute either the 'self' or an entity. The eighteen aspects of sense are, separately and together, void.

There is only 'Mind-Source', of absolute purity and without any limit of any kind.

According to Advaita, in the original state of the Totality of the potential or pure Subjectivity, there is an utter absence of objectivity; therefore, there can be no question of anyone or anything feeling the sense of being present. On that state of Unicity, the sense of Presence arises (I AM – Consciousness) and simultaneously brings forth upon Itself the totality of the manifestation, along with the concepts of space and time in which the phenomena can be extended.

This Impersonal Consciousness upon which the phenomenal manifestation takes place is 'pure knowledge'; ignorance is that state when the Impersonal Consciousness – I AM – after objectifying itself in the duality of manifestation as subject and object, becomes identified with each sentient being as the individual ego-doer, and the 'me'-concept is created – 'me' as opposed to the 'other'. It is this ego with the sense of personal doership that is the bondage from which liberation is sought.

Liberation is the realisation of Universal or Impersonal Consciousness as our true nature: the phenomenal object with which Consciousness has identified itself is mainly an aberration or an illusion, merely an appearance which cannot possibly have any independent nature of its own.

Identification with a separate body-mind organism as a separate entity through conceptualising may be considered as ignorance; so it might be assumed that with the dawn of the Ultimate Understanding, not only ignorance but even the bondage of conceptualising is annihilated. But the problem is that while in ignorance the individual identified himself with the body, after the ignorance is gone, he identifies himself with the *Brahman*, the Impersonal Consciousness, and says "I am Brahman." But underneath both identities hides the real culprit, the autonomous individual. Any gain is no gain at all if it is still in the realm of duality and conceptualising.

An average individual is firmly identified with his body and is totally ignorant about his true nature. Identification with the body is so firmly entrenched that it prevails not only in the waking state but also in the dream state and the deep sleep state. The three states of Consciousness are identified, in Advaita, with the three states of speech: *vaikhari* (the spoken word) with the waking state, *madhyama* (the stage of thinking prior to the sound of the spoken word) with the dream state, and *pashyanti* (the stage of subconscious thinking) with deep sleep. The fourth state is *paraa* (the thought I AM), which is associated with the Impersonal Consciousness.

The depth of the body-identification is seen from the fact that the sleeper wakes up even from deep sleep when called upon by name loudly enough. When the deep understanding happens, there is firm disidentification in all the three states of Consciousness. That the individual *jiva* is supposed to become one with *Shiva* through disciplinary practices, according to established belief, is rather inaudacious because the *jiva* has always been one with *Shiva*, and there can be no question of 'acquiring' any oneness with *Shiva*. All that happens is that the individual instead of believing that he is the body, now believes "I am Brahman." Actually, our true nature is That which has been prior to both knowledge and ignorance. Any disciplinary effort would necessarily involve a conceptual 'me', the pseudo-subject which itself is the basic cause of the conceptual bondage.

To return to the basics, there is only the Infinite, Intemporal Absolute – totally unconditioned, extremely devoid of any identity or attribute and thus not aware of Itself. The very thought of awareness, of a 'me' – totally different from 'I' as the Absolute – is instant bondage whose duration is identical with that of the conceptual 'me'. Thus, bondage is purely conceptual and consequently so is the freedom from this concept of bondage.

The concept of a 'me' comes into existence when the Universal, Impersonal Consciousness objectifies Itself into the manifestation as phenomena, and identifies Itself with each human phenomenon as the subject of all objects. This pseudo-subjectivising of pure Subjectivity, regarding It as a 'me', is specifically what constitutes bondage. The 'me'-concept as the individual doer itself is the bondage from which liberation is sought.

The bondage consists of the assumption of being the subject of the objects perceived. In other words, the bondage is simply considering the subject-object and the object-object as real and separate, and, of course, liberation consists of the re-establishment of both as mere conceptual appearances instead of 'Reality'. Liberation really consists in realising there never was any bondage because there never was any separate entity-doer to be bound.

12. There is sensual eating and wise eating. When the body suffers the pangs of hunger and is provided with food that is necessary, it is called wise eating. On the other hand, providing food based on greed and gluttony, delight being taken in the flavours and the variety, you are permitting the distinctions which arise from wrong, mistaken thinking. Seeking to gratify the organ beyond the necessary quality and quantity – is called sensual eating.

The six senses must necessarily be used in daily living in the ordinary course, but using them for sensual delight, beyond what is necessary for one's well-being, would not be right.

The various events in one's daily living do not exist, according to Advaita, other than as movements in Consciousness. The essential difference between the ordinary person and the apparently Self-realised person is that the ordinary person reacts to all events, decides which ones are pleasant and which ones are not, and pursues the pleasant ones and tries to avoid the unpleasant ones. The apparently Self-realised person lives non-volitionally and accepts events as they happen as God's Will and according to the Cosmic Law.

For all practical purposes, in the eyes of the beholder, there is no apparent difference between an ordinary person and an apparently Self-realised person in the actual experience of the usual sense objects, but there is a basic difference in their respective *attitudes*. Both body-mind organisms have natural preferences, based on genes and conditioning; both enjoy the experience when the preference is satisfied, but if the preference is not satisfied the apparently Self-realised person accepts the situation, while the ordinary person pursues his preferences and experiences frustration.

In other words, the apparently Self-realised person does not hanker after more pleasure in daily living, nor does he resist whatever comes his way as sense objects. Wanting something positively or not wanting something negatively are both aspects of volition, and in the case of the apparently Self-realised person there is absolutely no volition. His sensorial apparatus responds to an external stimulus without the intervention of the mind. He lives his life 'like a dry leaf in the breeze'. He knows that his life is being lived according to God's Will or the Cosmic Law, like everyone's life, and merely witnesses life happening naturally.

13. Those who seek enlightenment through hearing the Dharma – known as Shravakas ("the one who hears") – allow concepts to arise in their mind, instead of seeking intuitive knowledge by eliminating conceptualising in the mind. They may attain to Buddhahood only after an infinitely long duration. The Supreme Way is to awaken suddenly to the fact that your own Mind is the Buddha, that there can be nothing to be obtained or even a single deed to be performed.

The students of the Way have to realise that getting involved in a single thought could raise a barrier between the Way and yourself. To be a Buddha means no objectivising from thought-instant to thought-instant, no activity from thought-instant to thought-instant. You need study no doctrines whatsoever but only learn to avoid seeking anything or getting attached to anything.

That which is neither born nor destroyed is the Buddha. Mind is unborn when nothing is sought; Mind is not destroyed when there is no attachment to anything.

The eighty-four thousand methods for dealing with the eighty-four thousand forms of delusion are merely figures of speech to attract people toward the Gate, but the fact of the matter is that not a single one of them have any real existence. The Dharma means relinquishment of everything, including the Dharma itself!

"Huang Po sometimes implies that Hinayana followers also pay too much attention to the literal meaning of the scriptures, thereby not being able to be open to intuitive knowledge through eliminating conceptualising. Those who are able to avoid conceptualising do not need the scriptures at all."*

According to Advaita, the Source is the potential plenum, pure Subjectivity, totally untouched by objectivity, and It

* From Blofeld's footnotes to the original text.

therefore cannot be conceived as an object. Phenomenally it cannot be conceived and from the noumenal point of view, it is the very source of phenomenal conceptuality.

Noumenon is the eternal Subject, the cause and the source of all phenomena. It cannot be affected by either space or time, which are both conceptual aspects of manifestation. What is more, even considering it as 'IT' or 'Subjectivity' is also a concept. This inconceivable state can only be 'conceived' as 'I' – a non-entity, eternally present.

The most important consequential corollary of this concept of 'I' as the eternal Source-Subject is that all of the interrelated opposites – the seer and the seen, the hearer and the heard, the hater and the hated, the lover and the loved – are all objects within phenomenal duality. This is the real basis of *bhakti*: the worshipper and the worshipped are dual only in phenomenality, but as the 'I'-Subject, they both can only be the noumenal Unicity.

The Unicity of the potentiality, the 'I'-Subject, gets dichotomised in the mechanism of manifestation as subject and object, although all are phenomenal objects in manifestation. When the Ultimate Understanding – metanoesis or *para-vritti* – occurs, the pseudo-subject ceases to be an object. It becomes void by the superimposition of the opposites and through this void returns to the original potentiality, the 'I'-Subject. It is understood, of course, that this itself is a concept – only a pointer – because phenomenally this potentiality can only be total absence, and noumenally it can only be total Presence.

The objective void is the subjective plenum; the objective nothingness is the subjective fullness.

The 'I'-Subject cannot be comprehended because other than the 'I'-Subject, there cannot be any comprehender! This total potentiality, the noumenal 'I'-Subject, by its very nature is incognisable, like a mirror which reflects but does not retain. It is incognisable precisely because 'It' is all that we all are.

14. All that the students of the Way need to remember, in order to be successful, is not to get attached to any single thing beyond the Mind.

To say that the real Dharmakaya of the Buddha – the highest of the three Bodies, synonymous with the Absolute – resembles the Void is another way of saying that the Dharmakaya is the Void, and the Void is the Dharmakaya – they are one and the same. But if you define that Dharmakaya as something existing, then it is not the Void; and if you define the Void as something existing, then it is not the Dharmakaya.

Therefore, refrain from any objective conception of the Void or the Dharmakaya. These two do not differ from each other. Nor is there any difference between Buddhas and sentient beings, or between Nirvana and samsara, or between Bodhi and delusion. Ordinary people look to their surroundings while the true seekers look to Mind, but the true Dharma is to ignore them both.

Human beings are afraid to forget their minds, being afraid of falling through the Void with nothing to hold on to, because of their ignorance that the Void is not really void but the realm of the real Dharma: the spiritually enlightening nature that is without beginning, as ancient as the Void, subject neither to birth nor death, neither existing nor not existing, neither pure nor impure, neither young nor old, neither silent nor clamorous, having neither size nor form, neither colour nor sound, and occupying no space.

This spiritually enlightening nature cannot be sought, or comprehended, or explained in words, or materially contacted, or achieved by meritorious deeds. This nature is Mind, the Buddha, the Dharma, shared by all the Buddhas and Bodhisattvas, together with all things possessed of life. This is the truth and any other thought would be wrong. Therefore, immediately refrain from all conceptualising. Only a total, tacit understanding is necessary: any mental process must lead to error. All there is, is a transmission of Mind by Mind. Be careful not to look outward to material surroundings: that would be like mistaking a thief for your son, giving him a warm welcome and enabling him to sneak away with your most valuable possession – the key to the riddle of life which unlocks the gate of Nirvana.

According to Advaita, *Shiva* and *Shakti* are essentially the same. The manifested universe, being the mirrorisation or objectivisation of the Unmanifest, cannot be anything different from the Unmanifest. Although phenomena are sensorially perceptible and, therefore, 'present' or 'real', the noumenon (being the potential plenum) must necessarily be the Absolute Absence on which the presence of phenomenality appears. At the same time Advaita describes the indescribable in terms which show that *Sat-Chit-Ananda*, the three-in-one aspect of the unmanifest potential, is in direct contrast to the relevant aspects of the manifest universe.

The simple explanation is that this description would certainly not be necessary if the essential identity between the interrelated opposites had been perceived by the seeker. It so happens, however, that we identify ourselves with what-we-think-we-are – individual phenomenal entities. We think in terms of a cogniser and the object cognised as being things with substance – real. Such thinking clouds the fact that what-we-ARE is not an object but pure Subjectivity: the cognise-ING, the function-ING of the total manifestation. Both the cogniser and the cognised object are essentially mere appearances or hallucinations in the totality of the manifestation, the objectivisation of the only Subject. The consequence of this mistaken identity is bondage – suffering – misery from which liberation is sought. It is against this background of bondage and suffering that the concept of *Sat-Chit-Ananda* has been put forth.

We are conditioned to consider 'real' as only that which can be sensorially perceived, but the fact of the matter is that whatever is sensorially perceivable is phenomenal: merely an appearance extended in space (for the three-dimensional volume) and extended in duration (so that what is extended in space may be perceived and measured). This very factor about a phenomenon makes it an object that is subject to age and change i.e. *asat*, as opposed to the Unmanifest Absolute which is *Sat* (changeless, eternal Beingness). It is thus that the temporal universe and Intemporality would appear to be different and opposite, though in fact they are not. Intemporality *is* the temporal universe, but it is not sensorially perceptible because it is not extended in space-time. The Intemporal, the Unmanifest, is not an object but pure Subjectivity. No objective attributes such as conceptuality or affectivity can be applied to it.

When 'I', pure Subjectivity, remains in the intemporality of the presence of each *Kshana* (generally understood as a split-second, but strictly, "the 90th part of a thought, the 4500th part of a minute, during which 90 people are born and as many die"), there can be no objective duration in which to experience either pain or pleasure, and equanimity prevails. But when the *Kshanas* get horizontally connected into duration, the subjective Whole-Mind gets split into objective temporality and the duality of subject-object: 'me' and the 'other'.

Only an object can suffer; all phenomena are objects and, therefore, susceptible to suffering. Noumenon, being Subjectivity, is invulnerable to suffering and is, therefore, *Ananda*, happiness through peace of mind – *Sukha-Shanti*. The sentient being is identified consciousness, but fundamentally is Consciousness as Subjectivity. The ego, the individual entity, forgets this basic fact and, therefore, suffers bondage. Not subject to time and space, and not perceptible to the senses, 'me' and the 'other' are both the

Noumenon, the Impersonal Consciousness that is the Subject of time and space. But, all that is perceptible to the senses is the phenomenon that the 'me' thinks he is. This is the main reason for the concept of *Sat-Chit-Ananda*: to remind the individual entity of his origin.

15. 'Abstinence', 'calm' and 'wisdom' exist only because of the existence of 'greed', 'anger' and 'ignorance'. Thus, without illusion, how can there be Enlightenment? Therefore, Bodhidharma said, "The Buddha enunciated all Dharma in order to eliminate every vestige of conceptual thinking. If I totally refrained from conceptual thinking, would there be any use of the Dharma?"

Therefore, all that is necessary is to attach yourselves to nothing but the original source of all things: the pure Buddha-Nature.

If the Void could be adorned with countless jewels, would they remain in position? The Buddha-Nature is the Void, and if you were to adorn it with inestimable merit and wisdom, they would not remain there; all they would do is to conceal its original Nature and make it invisible. Certain Buddhist sects attach great importance to the acquisition of merit and knowledge, but this implies a dualistic concept of Reality which the Zen teaching considers to be an insurmountable obstacle to the realisation of the One Mind.

Zen Buddhism warns against another type of dualism – that which is called the Doctrine of Mental Origins. This doctrine postulates that all things are built up in Mind and that they manifest themselves upon contact with the external environment, and cease being manifest when that environment is not present. But it is not correct to conceive of an environment that could be separate from the pure, unvarying nature of all things in the Mind.

There is a warning against another sect: the Mirror of Concentration and Wisdom. This requires the use of sight, hearing, feeling and cognising, which lead to successive states of calm and agitation. But these involve conceptions based on environmental objects; they are temporary expedients pertaining to the lower categories of 'roots of goodness'. Roots of goodness are believed by those sects to be 'Enlightenment potentials' of varying degrees of strength with which individuals are reborn in accordance with the varying merits gained in former lives.

This category of 'roots of goodness' merely enables people to understand what is said to them. If you wish to *experience*, you must not indulge in such conceptions. They are all environmental Dharmas concerning things which are and things which are not, based on existence and non-existence.

Avoid concepts of existence and non-existence concerning everything, and then you will *apperceive* the Dharma.

According to Advaita, one's real nature is neither knowledge nor ignorance, both being interrelated concepts, but pure Wisdom, beyond all conceptualisation. There is neither an objective nor a subjective self; there is only non-objectivity.

Phenomenally, the subject-object relationship is the duality of 'self' and the 'other', the dual aspects of the concept whose source is the Noumenon. Objects are non-existent since they have no existence or nature independent of their noumenal Source. This means that the subject (in the subject-object relationship) is also non-existent and, therefore, there is really no question of any subject perceiving its objects. There is only pure see-ING as the functional aspect of the objectivisation of the Noumenon.

The very idea of seeing one's true nature is based on a cogniser cognising the true nature of the cogniser himself. The idea of true nature is itself a concept, as is the idea of a cogniser, because he would be the conceiver of the concept. How then can a concept cognise another concept? The real realisation can only be that what-one-IS is the absence of 'oneself' as an autonomous entity with volition: total absence of the notion (or cognition) of the absence of himself. In other words, it is only in the total absence of oneself that there can be total presence of what-one-IS.

The idea of a seeker is based on a 'me' thinking, doing, worshipping, meditating etc. whereas metanoesis or *para-vritti* happens spontaneously; there is no 'who' to achieve it by means of personal effort. All that one can do is perhaps to prepare the necessary conditions for its happening by the surrender of one's doership, which is tantamount to disidentification with the phenomenal autonomous entity. In other words, it must be apprehended that all phenomenal events (including efforts to seek out one's true nature) constitute only a shadow-play. What-we-ARE is that noumenality which enables us as sentient beings to apprehend anything at all. Indeed, *we are that apprehending itself* (without the conceptual duality of the apprehender and that which is apprehended). Apprehending, as such, is the functioning aspect of the objective expression of the noumenal and, therefore, is noumenal in nature.

The traditional Hindu concept of the individual merging with *Shiva*, the Noumenon, implies an essential duality between that-which-we-think-we-are and That-which-we-ARE, whereas this duality is purely conceptual, like that of the wave and the water; the wave and the water do not need to be joined, the wave merely subsides into water.

Where bondage and freedom are concerned, it is really a matter of negation – abandoning something rather than doing something positive, because even these are themselves concepts intimately involved with the illusion of the individual. Or, more accurately, it is neither a matter of doing something nor of not doing something, but of merely SEEING things as they are, BEING what we ARE, LIVING as what-we-ARE. In such SEEING – BEING – LIVING, there is no 'who' at all, only noumenal living – enlightened living.

So long as there is a 'me' thinking, feeling and reacting as an autonomous, independent entity, there cannot be any difference between ignorance and enlightenment. Both would be interrelated concepts applied to another concept, the individual. When the individual entity is seen for what it is – a mere appearance – ignorance cannot remain, and where there is no ignorance, there is no need for any knowledge or enlightenment.

16. From the time when Bodhidharma arrived in China, it is said that he spoke only of the One Mind and transmitted only the one Dharma, never speaking of any other Dharma. That Dharma was the wordless Dharma, and that Buddha was the intangible Buddha, since they were in fact Pure Mind, the source of all things. This is the only Truth. Prajna is wisdom; wisdom is the formless original Mind-Source.

A student of the Way, by involving himself in even a single samsaric thought, falls among devils. If he gets involved in a single thought leading to dualistic perception, he falls into heresy. To hold that there is something born and to try to eliminate it, is to fall among the Shravakas: "Hinayanists who are dualists in as much as they seek to overcome their samsaric life in order to enter Nirvana; while Zen does not accept samsara as other than Nirvana."*

To hold that things are not born but capable of destruction is to fall among the followers of the Middle Vehicle. Nothing is born and nothing is destroyed. Away with your dualism, your preferences and dislikes. Every single thing is just the One Mind. When you have perceived this, you will have mounted the chariot of the Buddhas.

According to Advaita, the very first thought is the arising of Consciousness – I AM – and this thought is impersonal, direct and immediate (there is no question of ignorance or knowledge). It is the objectivisation of what-we-ARE. This impersonal thought makes for living without identification with any separate doer-entity. The other kind of thought, totally different, arises after Consciousness has identified with a particular form as a separate suppositionally subjective entity; it is in this identified entity that the questions of ignorance and knowledge, bondage and liberation arise. Any thought proceeding through the intermediary of such an

* From Blofeld's footnotes to the original text.

entity objectivises everything all the time because that is its nature and function. Such thought, however, can only create bondage because it is not an objectivisation of what-we-ARE: it is the separation, due to volition, of 'self' and the 'other', which is the basis of ignorance and knowledge.

Once thinking as an individual ceases, after the total surrender of volition and doership, objectivisation also ceases because everything is seen as a happening according to God's Will/the Cosmic Law, and neither ignorance nor knowledge has any significance.

There is a significant distinction between knowledge and knowing. It may be subtle but it is clear – knowledge comes from outside, knowing is within. Knowledge, as the interrelated opposite of ignorance, is in the realm of temporal conceptualising whereas knowing is direct, intuitive, without any intermediacy of thinking. One does not say "I think I am alive and present here." One *knows*.

Where there is knowing, knowledge disappears. It would be useless for anyone to go to a guru without leaving his 'luggage of conceptualising' elsewhere. It is only a vacant or fasting mind – and, therefore, an alert mind – in which 'Knowing' can happen.

17. People feel desire and hatred because they indulge in conceptual thinking based on phenomenal objects. If conceptual thinking ceases, phenomenal objects become void. But if you try to eliminate phenomena without first stopping conceptual thinking, you will not only fail but intensify its power to disturb you.

In other words, all things just do not exist, and all there is, is intangible Mind. There is only one Reality, neither to be realised nor attained. To believe that you are able to realise something or attain something is to be arrogant. The men who flapped their garments and left the meeting as mentioned in the Lotus Sutra were those who thought they had understood all that there was to be understood, and were smugly satisfied.

Therefore, the Buddha said, "I truly obtained nothing from Enlightenment." There is just a mysterious tacit understanding and no more.

ॐ

The very core of the Advaita teaching is contained in what the sage Ashtavakra has said:

"If you detach yourself from the identification with the body, and remain relaxed in and as Consciousness, you will, this very moment, be happy, at peace and free from bondage."

The sage had realised that his royal disciple, King Janaka, was at a stage of spiritual advancement where a certain block had developed and that block could only be removed by a powerful blasting. And what is said in this verse did exactly that: the sudden transformation of King Janaka into the Final Understanding, the ultimate *Knowing*.

The words "remain relaxed in and as Consciousness" form the very basis of the Advaita teaching. There is no prescription of any rigorous set of practices and disciplines. All it needs for *enlightenment to happen* is a clear understanding and acceptance of a dimension totally different from intellectual comprehension. What intellectual comprehension brings about is a belief in what is comprehended, but an intuitive apperception is based on faith that is confirmed in the experience of life. Intellectual comprehension is based on argumentation, logic, effort and conflict. Intuitive apperception is based on a certain inescapable inevitability, a relaxed acceptance of 'what-is', totally free of any doubt or opinion.

18. If an ordinary man, when he is about to die, could see the five elements of Consciousness as void, the four physical elements as not constituting the individual entity, the Real One Mind as formless and neither coming nor going, his nature as something not beginning with his birth and ending with death, but as all whole and motionless in its beingness, his Mind and all the objects as One – he would receive enlightenment in a flash. He would no longer be involved in the Triple World, and would not be concerned with rebirth.

If he were to behold the wonderful sight of all the Buddhas welcoming him, surrounded by various wonderful phenomenal objects, he would be totally unconcerned. On the other hand, he would experience no terror if he were to see all sorts of horrible forms in front of him.

He would be totally oblivious of all conceptualisation and totally one with the Absolute unconditioned Being.

Man wants to know the meaning and significance of life and death. The beautiful flower that blooms in the wilderness for a brief period of time is as much a part of the manifested universe as is man. The flower is not concerned with the meaning of its existence, nor is the wild beast in the jungle worried about the significance of life and death, although it is as much a sentient being as a man. The seeking of meaning is a function of the mind-intellect and, therefore, different people find different meanings in the same things.

What happens after death? We must obviously be in the same state that we were in before life started in the womb: we would return to the Source, the perennial potential plenum. Nature would proceed in any case along its normal course. If the intellect is stopped from conceptualising, and thus from interfering with the natural fluidity of the mind, we would be free of unnecessary harrowing anticipations. It is certainly possible for the horror of the concept of death to be absent from consciousness, but it is not possible to do so deliberately and purposefully because the mind (the contents of Consciousness) is persistent about something that it wants to avoid. It can happen only when the sense of personal doership has been uprooted from the ego.

According to Advaita, the personality of any future birth will be drawn from the totality of the Universal Consciousness in which is collected all the 'clouds of images' that keep on being continuously generated. This total collection gets distributed among new births as they are being created, with certain characteristics that will produce precisely those actions which are necessary according to the script of the divine playwright. No individual need been concerned as a separate individual entity with any previous personality.

In this temporal dream play where sentient beings are created and destroyed in thousands every minute, evolution must obviously form the basis of the play of *Nisarga* (Life and Living). In the physicist's bubble chambers, science tells us *infinitesimally* small high-energy elementary particles (many of which are supposed to have a lifetime shorter then a millionth of a second!) collide and annihilate each other or create new particles that give rise to a fresh chain of events in manifestation. Similarly, every baby born would be expected to play a particular role in the living dream play, so that the play may proceed on its inevitable course, according to the divine script.

The sentient being, which as a mere appearance in Consciousness cannot possibly have independent choice of action, is created in order to fulfil a particular function (whether as a Hitler or a Churchill, or an insignificant individual), and not the other way around. It is not that a new function is created just so that the individual animus be punished or rewarded for his *karma* in a previous birth!

The supposed individual entity in any case is not an independent, autonomous entity – he merely carries out his destined function which paves the way for the destined function of another supposed individual in the temporal future, according to the divine script of the dream play. There would necessarily be continuity between the form that dies and the new form that is born because evolution goes on, and nature does not start from scratch each time. This is obviously why Mozart could compose music when he was twelve and the sage Jnaneshwar could produce the saintly *Jnaneshwari* at the age of sixteen. But there is no question of a conceptual individual entity identifying himself with a series of births in the temporal manifestation.

On this point, the Buddha is supposed to have said what could be considered the last word:

"As there is no self, there is no transmigration of a self; but there are deeds and continued effects of deeds. These deeds are being done but there is no doer. There is no entity that migrates, no self is transferred from one place to another; but there is a voice uttered here and the echo comes back."

19. That which is called the City of Illusion contains the Two Vehicles, the Ten Stages of a Bodhisattva's Progress, and the two forms of Full Enlightenment (including the form which leads to the awakening of others). All of them are powerful teachings for arousing people's interest, but they still belong to the City of Illusion – a term from the Lotus Sutra, implying temporary or incomplete Nirvana; but according to the Zen view all these teachings are likely to lead their followers to the City of Illusion because all of them subscribe to some form or other of dualism.

That which is called the 'Place of Precious Things' is the real Mind, the treasure of our own real Nature, which cannot be measured or accumulated. But where is the 'Place of Precious Things'? It obviously is a place to which no directions can be given because then it would be a place in space. In other words, it cannot be precisely described or located, but it is there when you have the tacit Ultimate Understanding.

The traditional Indian has been conditioned to believe that nothing can be acquired without personal effort and hard work, and this indeed is so in daily living. But where enlightenment is concerned he has to forget whatever he has learnt; he must understand that there is no qualitative difference between pleasure, work and meditation. Real quietude, true happiness, consists not in volitional effort to achieve happiness misunderstood as pleasures in life, but in understanding what Self-abidance is. Self-abidance is not something to be acquired by an individual entity but something which arises spontaneously when the mind is free of the concepts of right and wrong, the acceptable and the unacceptable, and all such pairs of opposites. Self-abidance or enlightenment is our natural state, and does not need to be acquired by any personal effort. Any personal, volitional effort only strengthens the ego, the 'me', which is itself the obstruction that covers and hides our original state. What is more, the true and total understanding of this very fact is all that is necessary for the seeker.

When the understanding is true and total, the question that usually bothers the seeker is seen as a joke. The question is: What do I have to *do* in order to have the total acceptance (and not merely the intellectual comprehension) that I am not the doer? Since you are not the doer, there is nothing you can do; it can only *happen* when it is supposed to happen, according to your destiny/God's Will/the Cosmic Law.

Specifically, what is the Ultimate Understanding? It would be difficult to give a more succinct answer than the statement of the Chinese sage Shou Hui: "Only by avoiding intentions will the mind be rid of objects." In other words, the total, Ultimate Understanding can only be that there cannot be any separate, individual entity with volition who can have intentions; therefore, there is nobody who can have the choice of decision and action. The apparent individual entity does not live his life but his life is being lived as an instrument through which Consciousness functions and brings about precisely what is supposed to happen according to the Cosmic Law.

20. Most of the students of the Way try to get Enlightened through the Dharma that is taught in words and not through the Dharma of Mind, and they are known as Ichhantikas or Shravakas or Pratyeka-Buddhas or Hearer-Buddhas. Even after eons of effort, they will not become attuned to the original Buddha-Essence.

Those who are not Enlightened from within their own Mind, but from hearing the Dharma that is taught in words, make light of Mind and attach importance to doctrine and, therefore, can only advance gradually.

It is only if you have a tacit understanding of Mind, that there will be no need for you to search for any Dharma at all, for then Mind *is* the Dharma.

True understanding comports the realisation that it is only the 'me'-notion, the ego, that can have any intention, volition or will. There is a misconception that the absence of intention or will or motivation implies inaction, but action cannot stop: it will be spontaneous noumenal action.

In the absence of any individual comprehender, the true understanding cannot be the result of effort by a non-existent doer; it can only be a spontaneous arising, a result of the natural tendency of the identified consciousness, that inherent urge towards disidentification.

As the sage Ashtavakra has put it, happiness belongs to none but the master-idler to whom even the natural action of opening and closing the eyes seems an affliction. What he obviously means to imply is that the continuous normal action of blinking, if regarded as a volitional act, would have been an affliction. The process of blinking, the respiratory process, the digestive process and the working of the incredibly complex nervous system are all involuntary functions in the human body-mind organism.

To the 'master-idler' all actions which take place through the body-mind organism are as involuntary as the other processes. He does not consider himself as the individual doer of any actions and is, therefore, referred to by the sage as the 'master-idler'. He merely witnesses everything that happens, without comparing and judging. All actions, including his own, are seen as being part of the functioning of Totality. Ramana Maharshi, the great master-idler, was once asked why he did not do some social service instead of merely lying about on his couch. The Maharshi calmly asked the questioner: "How do you know that all that is necessary is not already happening just through my being here?"

The more the seeker learns, the more he adds to the memory, the storehouse from which more and more conceptualising happens; these concepts add to the existing conditioning which covers the original state of Self-abidance, which means the absence of conceptualising. In those rare moments when the body is relaxed and the mind is quiescent, there exists a state in which the ego is extremely subdued, almost unaware. Unawareness of the identified consciousness, the ego, means the Awareness of the Self, the Impersonal Consciousness.

In everyday living the human being mistakenly believes he has the effective choice of decision and action, and spends a lot of energy worrying about results. The sage Ashtavakra says that the man of wisdom is free from opposites like 'this is done but that remains to be done'. True awareness of what remains to be done leads spontaneously to the necessary action, without the intervention of the mind worrying about it.

The man of wisdom does not worry about the results of his actions for two reasons: one, his actions are subject to the limitations of his natural characteristics – physical, mental and temperamental – with which the body-mind organism was infused at the moment of conception, and two, he is aware that the results of one's actions have never been in the control of any man.

It is the human mind-intellect which refuses to accept the natural interconnectedness of opposites as a fact of life. Life and death become life versus death; good and evil become good versus evil. And thus living becomes one continuous process of choice and the pursuit of that choice. The human being is trained and conditioned from his very infancy to choose one against the other, but the fact of the matter is that evil cannot be exterminated nor can disease be eradicated altogether; when one disease is eradicated, another quickly takes its place.

Happiness consists in accepting the principle of polarity, accepting that the interrelated opposites are the very basis of both the universe and the movements therein. As Lao Tzu has put it: "Knowing the male and keeping the female, one becomes a universal stream; becoming a universal stream, one is not separated from eternal virtue." 'Male and female' obviously refers to the dominant natural characteristics, like the inseparable poles of a magnet or the pulse and interval in any vibration.

Until comparatively recently, that is to say, until Newtonian physics (which prevailed for several centuries) was overthrown by modern physics, the idea of an inner unity of opposites was confined only to mystics, mostly Eastern. But now even science has accepted reality as a union of opposites. Thus, for instance, rest and motion are no longer opposites; according to the theory of relativity, 'each is both'. An object for one observer may be at rest whilst, at the same time, for another observer it may be in motion. Similarly, the separation between wave and particle had to disappear when it was found that in certain circumstances a wave could behave like a particle and vice versa – so now we have 'wavicles'. There is now no separation of mass from energy, and the old opposites are now seen as two aspects of one Reality. This discovery was actually experienced horrendously by the people of Hiroshima and Nagasaki.

21. Seekers thinking they are hindered by environmental phenomena try to escape from them in order to still their minds, or those who think that they are hindered by individual events from perceiving underlying principles try to obscure events in order to retain their grasp on principles. In doing so, they do not realise that what they are actually doing is to confuse phenomena for Mind, and events for principles.

Therefore, just let the mind become void and environmental phenomena will void themselves; let principles cease to stir and events will stop stirring themselves.

Many people are afraid to let their minds become empty because they are afraid of plunging into the void, but the fact of the matter is that it is their own Mind which is the void.

The ignorant eschew phenomena but not thinking; the wise eschew thinking and not phenomena.

Indian mystics have long held that a sudden spontaneous movement (I AM) in Consciousness-at-rest, not aware of Itself, gave rise to the entire manifestation as a block. Concurrent with that movement of Awareness, the potential Energy activated Itself, and since then nothing in the universe has been static. Things and events which appear to be separate and irreconcilable such as subject and object, past and future, cause and effect etc. are actually a single vibration. A wave cannot exist except as the unity of crest and trough. As Alfred North Whitehead has put it, "All elements in the universe exist as a vibratory ebb and flow of an underlying energy or activity." *Shakti* (Energy) is in constant movement.

The fact of the matter is that opposites do not really exist except as a concept. Man's unhappiness rests on the fact that he tries to eradicate one of the opposites – the ugliness, the evil, the weakness, the stupidity. The opposites are an illusion created by the mind-intellect through conceptual separation. When one thinks of beauty, the ugliness is already there; indeed, what is considered beautiful in one place or at one time is considered ugly at another.

As Omar Khayyam has put it:

"After a momentary silence spake
Some Vessel of a more ungainly Make;
'They sneer at me for leaning all awry:
What! did the Hand then of the Potter shake?'"

Ashtavakra says: "When the mind is free from pairs of opposites like 'this is done and that is not done', it acquires an indifference alike to righteousness, wealth, desire for sensual pleasure, *as well as liberation.*" Once the separation is seen as a mere concept, based on doership, all conceptual opposites lose their validity.

To quote Omar Khayyam again:

"There was the Door to which I found no Key;
There was the Veil through which I might not see;
Some little talk awhile of Me and Thee
There was – and then no more of Thee and Me."

In the absence of thee and me (as individual doers), in the absence of separation, lies true happiness. There is no subject seeking an object, or even anything called 'liberation'. Ashtavakra clearly tells us that happiness is not some *thing* which an individual can chase and acquire. True happiness exists simply when there is no conceptualising, no thinking.

22. The Bodhisattva has relinquished everything and does not even desire to accumulate merits.

There are three kinds of relinquishment:

a) The lowest form exists when various virtuous acts are performed in the hope of reward, even though one is already aware of the Dharma.

b) The medium form exists when the Way is followed by performing various acts without any hope of reward.

c) When everything has been relinquished: physical and mental, inside and outside, and no attachments of any kind exist; when action happens spontaneously, and when no distinction is made between subject and object, that is the highest form of relinquishment.

The first is a blazing torch held behind so that it cannot show the pitfalls in front; the second is like a blazing torch held to one side so that it is sometimes dark and sometimes light. The third is like a blazing torch held in the front which makes it impossible to mistake the path, without any pitfalls.

In a set of five verses, the sage Ashtavakra condenses the essence of Advaita as under:

a) Desire is at the root of ignorance, and so long as desire persists, the sense of the acceptable and the unacceptable, which is the sprout and branch of the tree of *samsara*, must necessarily continue.

b) Activity begets attachment, abstention from activity generates aversion. Rid of the bondage of opposites, the man of wisdom, established in the Self, lives like a child.

c) One who is attached to *samsara* wants to renounce it in order to free himself from misery, but one who is not attached continues to live in *samsara*, and yet lives happily.

d) He who seeks enlightenment as a seeker, and is still identified with the body as a doer, is neither a *jnani* nor a yogi, and suffers misery.

e) Unless everything is totally forgotten, you cannot be established in the Self, even if *Shiva*, *Krishna* or *Brahma* be your preceptor.

The acquiring of what seems acceptable has within itself the seed of the unacceptable because of the fear of losing it. In the case of physical illness, knowing the cause of it is half the solution. In the case of psychological illness – unhappiness – knowing the cause really needs no other positive action because it has no concrete basis.

It is a curious fact that a man goes to a guru, seeking some positive solution to get rid of the psychological illness of unhappiness. The joke is that the seeker with the psychological illness is seeking something more acceptable, and now there is a further seeking being done – for enlighten-ment. What Ashtavakra says is: give up all wanting; be satisfied with what-IS. The seeking, the frustration, will never cease through further seeking.

The past is dead and the future is non-existent. There is only the present moment, the eternal present moment from which can be witnessed the illusory movement of the future into the past. *The present moment is not between the future and the past, but is the constant timeless dimension, outside duration.* The flow of time cannot be witnessed except from a position outside of duration. It is stupid to live either in the frustration and successes of the past or in the projections of fears and hopes for the future. Remaining in the present moment, unconcerned with happiness or unhappiness, is the 'within' – the Kingdom of God, where there is nothing to be sought.

Finally, Ashtavakra asks the disciple to free himself from the ultimate bondage of the guru himself: "Unless everything (acquired phenomenally) is totally forgotten you cannot be established in the Self…" Zarathushtra gives his disciples the same message: "Whatever had to be said has been said; whatever had to be understood has been understood. Now forget whatever has been said. Forget everything I have said except this last message: Beware of Zarathushtra."

23. The mind of the Bodhisattva is like the Void in which everything is relinquished: thinking of the past, thinking in the present and thinking about the future – the total relinquishment of Triple Time.

Mind has always been transmitted with Mind and the Minds have been identical and do not differ. A transmission of the Void cannot be made through words; a transmission so made cannot be the Dharma. Transmitting and receiving transmission are a special kind of mysterious understanding with the result that not many have been able to receive it. The fact of the matter is, mind is not Mind and transmission is not transmission.

This is a reminder that all terms used in Zen are mere makeshifts.

As the sage Jnaneshwar has put it:

"The words that could describe the noumenal state have not been created, nor is the sight born which could perceive that state... That state is not such that it could be within the grasp of thought and words." If a person says he has slept well, the peace and contentment of that sleep spills over into this description of what he feels *now*; the word can only describe how he feels in the waking state. One cannot experience the sleeping state and, more accurately, 'one' does not exist in the sleeping state. Similarly, words can have significance only where objectivity is concerned. Thus, in phenomenality, the presence of noumenality can only be cognised as absence; since what-we-ARE is noumenal Presence, we cannot be sensorially aware of It as an object.

There is no difference between ignorance and knowledge (between ignorance and enlightenment) because in either condition it is the conceptual individual entity who experiences one or the other condition. In the noumenal state the individual entity disappears. So long as there is a 'me', thinking, feeling and reacting as an autonomous entity, there cannot be any difference between ignorance and enlightenment. When the individual entity is seen for what it is – a mere appearance – ignorance cannot remain, and there cannot be any need for enlightenment. It is the noumenal state which can only be *experienced* through Unicity.

The sage Jnaneshwar further says:

"Neither ignorance nor knowledge has any significance except in relation to each other, and when considered together they negate each other completely and nothing remains, thereby rendering both utterly useless... And thus what prevails is Impersonal Consciousness, the Source, I AM, and this swallows up both the concepts of ignorance and knowledge."

24. A Buddha is supposed to have three bodies: one, the omnipresent voidness of the real self-existent Nature of everything – the Dharmakaya; two, the underlying purity of all things – the Sambhogakaya; three, the Dharmas of the six practices leading to Nirvana and such other devices.

The Dharma of the Dharmakaya cannot be achieved through listening or reading; nothing can be said or made evident through words. There is only the omnipresent voidness of the real self-existent Nature of everything.

The Sambhogakaya and the Nirvanakaya cannot be considered a real Buddha or preacher of Dharma because spoken Dharmas which respond to events through the senses and in all sorts of forms cannot be the real Dharma.

The phenomenal manifestation as such is nothing but the objective expression of the only Subject that is the Noumenon. The individual perceiver or knower as an entity just does not figure in this objectivisation of the Absolute Subject except as the psychosomatic apparatus through which Consciousness operates as sentience. The individual entity, the ego, arises only because Consciousness has identified Itself with each such apparatus so that life, as we know it, could happen through inter-ego relationships.

What is necessary to remember – and this happens spontaneously and naturally after Self-realisation – is the fact that objects as such, sentient or otherwise, can have no existence other than as mere appearances in Consciousness. As the sage Jnaneshwar says, "Now the smell has become that which smells; the hearing has become that which hears; the breeze has become the fan, the head has become the flowers which adorn it; the tongue has become the lusciousness of the juice; the lotus has become the sun and bloomed forth; the flowers have become the bee; the young woman has become the male who enjoys her female charms; just as a piece of gold is moulded into a lovely ornament, so the seeing itself has been transformed into the phenomenal manifestation.

Thus, the one who enjoys and that which is enjoyed are the enjoying; the one who perceives and that which is perceived are the seeing. *The enjoying and the seeing are the aspects of the Unicity in its objectification.*"

In other words, all perception, as such, is only a reflection in Consciousness, a pure mirrorisation, and the supposed entity through which the perception happens is nothing but a *tabula rasa,* a phenomenal 'reagent apparatus' with certain characteristic reactions. So, in the state of Self-realisation, *all perception remains as pure mirrorisation without any reactive interpretation.*

Even when new and fresh experiences are noticed in the life of a Self-realised person, they are not experienced by him as volitional experiences because he lives in a non-volitional way. The essential difference between the ordinary person and the Self-realised one (of course, strictly speaking, there is no 'one' as such) is that the ordinary person reacts to all events, decides which ones are pleasant and which are not, and strives to pursue the pleasant ones and avoid the unpleasant ones. The Self-realised person, living non-volitionally, lives in the present moment and accepts events as they occur.

Realisation of the absurdity of independent choice by an illusory 'me' naturally results in two things: one, there is total acceptance that it is the supposed 'volition', the exercise of choice and decision, that is the cause of the supposed bondage; and two, the abandonment of this apparent volition, which is worthless both in theory and practice. Thereafter, functioning in life means seeing, hearing, tasting, smelling, feeling and thinking, without any objective 'me' doing anything.

25. The term *unity* – a homogeneous spiritual brilliance – refers to the One Mind, which separates into six harmoniously blended 'elements', or the six sense organs. The six sense organs each become united with their relevant objects – the eyes with form, the ears with sound, the nose with smell, the tongue with taste, the fingers with touch, and the thinking mind with other entities. Between these six organs and their objects arise the six sensory perceptions, making the eighteen realms in all.

If you are able to understand that these eighteen realms have no objective existence, you will bind the six harmoniously blended 'elements' into a single spiritual brilliance which is the One Mind. But seekers cannot avoid forming concepts of 'a single spiritual brilliance' and the 'six harmoniously blended elements' – this is the reason they are chained to remaining as entities and fail to achieve the tacit understanding of the Original Mind.

The sage Jnaneshwar explains that all experiencing is impersonal ("Thou art the doer and Thou art the experiencer"):

"Senses, according to their nature, may run towards objects which satisfy them, but almost simultaneously there is the realisation that the experience is not different from what he (the Self-realised person) himself is – just as when the sight meets the mirror, almost simultaneously there is the realisation that the image therein is not different from the face."

For all practical purposes, in the eyes of the beholder, there is no apparent difference between an ordinary person and a Self-realised one as concerns the experience of the usual sense objects, but there is a fundamental difference in their attitudes.

While speaking of an experience, there is the habit to regard it as an event in itself, but what is known as an experience is nothing but a reaction to an outside stimulus, which is stored in memory as pleasant or unpleasant. In other words, an experience is not factual but only conceptual. It is important to remember that the experiencer in life is always the phenomenal 'me', the personal entity. But the Self-realised person considers it not as *his* experience but simply as *an* experience.

In other words, the experience-ING of pleasure or pain is considered by the man of wisdom as part of the functioning of Totality. It is only when the experiencing is interpreted through the dualistic process of a subject-object relationship that the experience loses its impersonal, intemporal element of functioning and assumes the duality of objectivisation.

Thus:

a) Three different kinds of gold ornaments may have three different shapes and three different names, but all three are the same basic metal, gold;

b) You will have three different sensorial experiences of touch, sight and taste, but the object will be the same: camphor. The essential element is its fragrance. Similarly, whatever the experiences, all of them happen in consciousness, never when you are in deep sleep or under sedation.

Therefore, the moment the senses go forth to meet their respective objects, in the Self-realised state the experience is realised for what it is: a manifestation in Consciousness, not based on a subject-object relationship. After Self-realisation, phenomena are seen as nothing but the Noumenon; such seeing is like seeing ourselves in the mirror of Consciousness.

An important distinction needs to be made between a biological reaction in the body-mind organism and an egoic reaction. When the eyes see something or the ears hear something or any other sense meets its object, there is an immediate reaction, which is actually a biological reaction based on the genes and conditioning in the body-mind organism. The man of wisdom is very clear about this and, therefore, does not feel that someone is angry or someone else is afraid, whereas the ordinary person does, and judges that someone accordingly.

It is necessary to understand that the biological reaction is a tendency, but whether it prevails on a particular occasion or not is an event over which the individual has no control. Therefore, if a sage is asked what he would do in any set of circumstances, his only answer would be: "I do not know what will happen." This means it is beyond his control, and he is not concerned. Ramana Maharshi was once asked whether only important events were predestined. His answer was "Everything!"

26. The Tathagata wished to preach the Simple Vehicle of Truth, but he knew that if he did so, people would not have been able to accept it, so out of compassion for those who would have scoffed at his teaching and continued to be immersed in the sea of samsara, he adopted the expedient of preaching that there are three vehicles.

There is, however, only One-Vehicle Way, and there is no way for describing the Dharma of the One Mind. So the Tathagata called Kashyapa to come and sit with him, and separately entrusted to him the wordless Dharma of the One Mind – to be separately practiced, and those who were destined to be Enlightened would accept the One Dharma.

In the Hindu philosophy, the attributes of the Absolute are *Sat-Chit-Ananda. Sat* means 'Being', *Chit* means 'Consciousness', and *Ananda* means 'peace of mind', though it is sometimes misconceived as 'bliss'. These are the three attributes of Brahman, as described by the Vedas (revealed Knowledge). They are not to be considered separately because even in their entirety they do not affect Brahman. Just as the sage Jnaneshwar has put it – the poisonous nature of poison does not affect the poison itself. Beingness and Consciousness finally end in the ultimate peace of mind in the Absolute state – transcending as it does the experiences, the experienced peace and the experiencing – annihilating the first two aspects and thus making the words *Sat* and *Chit* useless.

Relatively speaking, the expression *Sat-Chit-Ananda* could be conceptualised as: on the *Sat*, the Consciousness-at-rest, spontaneously arises the *Chit*, the movement I AM, together with the manifested universe. The realisation of the basic identity of the two – the Unmanifest Unicity and the multiplicity of the manifest universe – results in PEACE. The significance of this wonderful concept is that the realisation of phenomenality being merely the objectification of noumenality and, therefore, not an independent separate thing, breaks the duality, the separation between the 'me' and the 'other'. And this is what results in peace.

Words have to be used to try to describe the indescribable, or at least point to it, to reveal the nature of Brahman and destroy ignorance of it. They become the mirror to the Unmanifest and indicate the nature of what is sensorially not perceptible. On the one hand, the word makes *Shiva* accept himself as an embodied entity, while it is, on the other hand, through the word that the individual sentient being comes to realise his real nature.

The word is basically verbalised thought and is therefore nothing but conceptualising in the duality of subject-object relationship, through the relativity of interdependent opposites or counterparts. The relative thought which finds its expression in the word has created the fictitious ego, comprehended in the form of a pseudo-subject in relation to a comprehended object, although actually both are objects in the manifestation. Having thus created the fictitious ego-doer, thought then proceeds to keep the ego subjected to the concepts of personal guilt and bondage, and finally takes on the magnanimous role of providing the ego with the means of acquiring liberation from the bondage!

The apperception of Truth – our real nature – can be neither conceptualised nor expressed as vocalised thought because both can only be products of the split-mind of subject-object in duality. Awakening can only *happen* spontaneously when the conceptual individual-doer is totally absent, in a kind of internal in-seeing devoid of all duality and temporality. It can only happen in the deepest abyss of negation, in the total absolute absence of both positive and negative volition, or of an individual 'me'.

27. The question usually is, "What is the Way and how should it be followed?" But the question really is, "What sort of *thing* do you suppose the Way to be and why should you wish to follow it?"

The instructions which the Masters seem to have given for dhyana-practice were meant for the dull-witted and are not to be relied upon. Men of high capacity would not seek from others but would seek within themselves and find nothing tangible. By truly accepting that there is nothing really to be sought at all you would save yourself a lot of unnecessary mental effort.

Not to seek is to rest tranquil, not to eliminate anything. If you just look at the void in front of you, can you ever produce it or eliminate it? The Void is both one and manifold. All that human beings do is form concepts and concepts are related to the seeker. When you get involved in feeling, wisdom is shut out.

Is the seeker mistaken in all the questions he asks? All you have to do is see, and understand what is. Where is the question of being mistaken? The Buddha, when questioned about such things as existence and non-existence, would merely say: "Not this, not this."

According to Advaita, 'Reality' is the unbroken whole.

Physical reality means the manifest universe and the physicists tell us that no object can be said to 'exist' unless it is observed. Thus, the manifest universe exists only as the functioning of 'life' as we know it, which depends entirely on interconnection, that is to say, interhuman relationships based on the interconnected opposites of every conceivable kind.

Modern physics tells us that access to the physical world is only through experience, through our interaction with it.

This is a fundamental assumption of 'complementarity', a concept developed by Niels Bohr to explain the wave-particle duality of light: wave-like characteristics and particle-like characteristics are obvious opposites, but both are necessary to understand light.

This means that life cannot exist without interconnected opposites. It would also mean that life can exist only through experience, and that a human being can exist only with the interconnected qualities of head and heart existing at the same time, through the principle of complementarity.

Is a particular human being 'good' or 'bad'? The programming in every human body-mind organism contains both aspects of being human – good and bad – and it is meaningless to ask whether a person is a good person or a bad person. It would depend upon what experiment is being used, which person he or she is interacting with in the existing circumstances – the experience.

Another important aspect of 'experience' is that the possibilities are often not restricted to either/or. In the world of symbols (material things taken to represent abstract things), everything can be either this or that, but where it is a matter of experience, there are usually more alternatives. There is a story of a visiting American being stopped by a group of masked gunmen during the Lebanese civil war. It was a critical situation in which the wrong word could have cost him his life. He was asked: "Are you a Moslem or a Christian?" For a moment he was speechless, but the fear of death suddenly broke through the illusion of the symbolic either/or, and he found himself saying, "I am a tourist."

Experience is a state of being; the description of a state of being is a symbol, a concept – they do not follow the same rules.

Modern physicists have just realised what Advaita philosophy realised hundreds of years ago: in order to understand Reality one has to give up the concept and the symbol and perceive directly the 'inexpressible nature of undifferentiated Reality'. This 'undifferentiated Reality' is the same Reality of which we are all born a part of, but is seen in a totally different way by the enlightened mystic from that of the ordinary person.

The physicist has now begun to see Reality as it has been seen for a long time by the mystic: there is only one Unicity; all the different parts of the universe are manifestations of the ONE whole Unicity of Reality. The physicist has found that something need not necessarily be either a wave or a particle: it can be both, a 'wavicle'. He also has found that any subatomic particle *anywhere in the universe* 'Knows' what goes on anywhere else! Subatomic particles seem to be doing exactly what the others are doing elsewhere, everywhere in the universe.

In fact, quantum mechanics sees subatomic particles as 'tendencies to exist or happen', expressed in terms of probabilities, and not as 'things' at all. Perhaps the physicist is coming to the conclusion which the mystic has always known: the ultimate 'stuff' of the universe is a no-thing, an illusion! In other words, it would seem that the universe is not a collection of separate parts, because the separate parts, including the human beings, do not exist independently of one another but are actually parts of "one all-encompassing organic pattern."

Thus, it would actually seem that the science of physics and the phenomenon of enlightenment may not be too far apart. Both have come to the conclusion that an experience and a description of that experience through symbols – the experiment and the result of it – have a totally different set of rules: electricity is what it does, it cannot be described; happiness is an experience, it cannot be described. The mystic finds problems explaining what enlightenment is; the physicist finds problems trying to explain subatomic phenomena. Neither can be visualised.

Where Reality is concerned, the mind has to be transcended. Reality has to be experienced, not understood. There can only be an Impersonal Awareness of Reality, manifested as the universe. The unbroken wholeness – "That-which-is-Here and Now" cannot be understood by a part of it. According to the physicist David Bohm: "We must turn physics around. Instead of starting with parts and showing how they work together (the Cartesian order), we start with the whole." Also, "Thus, one is led to a new notion of unbroken wholeness, which denies the classical idea of analysability of the world into separately and independently existing parts..."

Then again, what the 'Copenhagen Interpretation' brought out is that "the proper goal of science is to provide a mathematical framework for organising and expanding our experiences rather than providing a picture of some reality that could lie behind these experiences."

In 1964 Dr. J. S. Bell published mathematical proof of a strange 'connectedness' among quantum phenomena, which since then has been known as Bell's Theorem. The theorem, which he reworked and refined over the next ten years until its present form, is generally considered as perhaps the most important single work in the history of physics. The Theorem points directly to the experience of enlightenment in Eastern spirituality. According to the theorem, the principle of local causes, according to which what happens in one area is quite independent of what happens in a separate area, is false. This means that we live our lives "in a non-local universe, characterised by superlumind (faster than light) connections between apparently 'separate parts'."

Since almost everything in physics has rested upon the assumption that nothing can travel faster than the speed of light, one can imagine the turbulence caused by Bell's Theorem. It is perhaps a coincidence that in May/June 2000 there was a report in the media that research has revealed that energy has been discovered which travels perhaps even 300 times faster than light! If this is confirmed, the physicist is not too far away from the Eastern mystic: the past, present and future are all there like a completed movie. Subsequently, the physicist Stephen Hawking has confirmed that everything in the world is predetermined. As David Bohm has put it, one is led to a new notion of 'unbroken wholeness'.

The demolition of locality would also lead to the conclusion that free will is clearly an illusion, and it is meaningless to think anything like 'could this have been avoided if...' This is pure Advaita.

There is a peace invocation which precedes the Eesha Upanishad:

> "The invisible (Brahman) is the Whole;
> The visible (the manifestation) too is the Whole;
> From the Whole (Brahman),
> the Whole (the visible universe) has come."

28. The seeker, frustrated with the fact that the Master has refuted everything he has said, complains that the Master has done nothing to point out the true Dharma to the seekers.

The Master explains that there is no confusion in the Dharma but that the questions themselves produce confusion. He asks the seeker what sort of true Dharma he is seeking. He explains that all that is needed is to observe things as they are and not to pay any attention to other people, because there are some people, like mad dogs, barking at everything that moves; they even bark when the wind stirs among the grass and leaves, mistaking motions taking place within their minds for external independently moving objects.

Abiding in one's real nature is all that is necessary. You are the Noumenon, the Truth. To be told to do something would be misleading because it would imply that there is something to be 'acquired' by some 'one' through effort. But the individual who is supposed to make the effort just does not exist, he is an illusion, a myth. All there is, is the Noumenon within which has appeared the illusion of the phenomenal universe.

Effort contains the illusory desire on the part of the illusory individual to achieve an illusory goal. All that is necessary for the seeker to do is to turn his gaze inward, whereas all effort is necessarily diverted outward. Mind when turned inward ceases to conceptualise and that itself is tantamount to liberation.

The matter of conceptualising has been one of considerable confusion and misunderstanding. The question arises: If Consciousness has always been free and unfettered, why did It identify Itself with each body-mind organism, create Its own limitation and cause the trouble about bondage and liberation? There are two ways of looking at the matter and both perspectives dissolve the question itself. If Consciousness has always been unfettered, totally free, why should It not limit Itself and thereby engage Itself in the *lila* (entertainment) that this life is? Also, it is only through this division into a subject-object relationship that Consciousness can perceive and cognise the phenomenal universe that it has 'created' within Itself. One sentient being, as the subject, perceives the other sentient beings as objects, and this is the 'mechanism' for Consciousness to cognise the manifestation.

Bondage does not arise from the duality of subject-object relationship, which is the necessary mechanism for the cognition of phenomenality by the Universal Consciousness. The *lila* of the interrelationship between human beings which Consciousness provides within Itself, which causes the pleasure and pain to the supposed individuals, is not the result of the mechanism of *duality*, but arises through the operation of *dualism*. It is the dualism which makes each individual consider itself as a separate, autonomous entity, with personal doership, as the subject of all the other objects, that causes the bondage. The basic fact is that the Noumenon is the only Subject – indeed, pure Subjectivity – and all are objects. A body-mind organism can only 'live' according to its basic nature, its *dharma* and, therefore, every entity is 'being lived' and does not live its life.

29. It has, from the beginning, never been the teaching of Zen that man should seek for learning through conceptualising. 'Studying the Way' has been just a way of saying something to arouse the people's interest.

Study leads to the retention of concepts and so the Way has been totally misunderstood.

The Way is not something that exists. Called Mind, it is not something to be found inside, outside or in the middle because it is not located anywhere at all. Because people insisted on seeking for It empirically and fearing that they may lose all interest in it, and, on the other hand, seeing the misery of the seekers, the Buddhas appeared and they selected the name 'Way', although there is actually no road.

But it has always been said:

"When the fish is caught, we pay no
more attention to the trap."

The Way is reached and Mind is understood when the body and mind receive spontaneity. A monk is called shramana because he has penetrated the original source of all things.

The fruit of attaining the shramana stage is gained by putting an end to all anxiety, not through book-learning.

Understanding is spontaneous and noumenal – including the understanding that compulsive action is also spontaneous – when the ego truly accepts the actual position that there is really no power in the ego to 'do' anything, that it is merely an instrument through which events happen, precisely the way they do, according to God's Will or the Cosmic Law. This means that the human being does not live his life but his apparent life is being lived. This is the Ultimate Understanding, which leads finally to the apparent annihilation of the ego.

This understanding leads to what may be called non-volitional living. It means, in effect, that one begins to take life as it comes along, in a world which seems to have lost all its previous boundaries and barriers, so that there really is no need to avoid false thoughts or seek true ones. No effort is really necessary; all the effort that is necessary at any time happens by itself.

Non-volitional living means merely witnessing whatever happens through any body-mind organism as a happening that had to happen according to God's Will or the Cosmic Law, without judging or condemning anyone – neither oneself nor the other.

Understanding is always spontaneous and noumenal because it is actually an impersonal happening, not a happening which an individual person has achieved. As the Zen poem puts it: "You cannot have it by taking thought; you cannot seek it by not taking thought." This might seem to be an impossible impasse, but that is not so. Effort (or effort not to make an effort) is based on desire or volition, which itself is an aspect of the ego. It is the split-mind which sees the impasse as such, while spontaneity is synonymous with the absence of the split-mind. Spontaneity can arise only when the split-mind of subject-object has been abandoned and trust is put in the Whole Mind.

It is an everyday experience that when our conscious mind cannot provide an answer to a problem, the answer comes to us when we 'sleep on it', through the unconscious mind. There has to be a realisation of the limitations of the conscious mind so that we do not force ourselves to be unreasonably careful or overly conscious of the illusory 'me', the ego-doer; we keep the liberty to have trust in that final authority which makes the grass grow and our limbs and organs work by themselves. Otherwise, anxiety and self-consciousness will destroy that minimum sensitivity so necessary for decisions to arise.

What actually happens in life is that we attach undue importance to past conventions, to conscious thinking, to communication by linear signs and mathematical symbols, and not nearly enough to the intuitive 'feel'; far more to the central spotlight vision and not enough to the peripheral vision. What happens now most of the time is that the conditioning of conventionality is so powerful that it smothers spontaneity. What is necessary is certainly not a surrender to a mad urge of caprice, but a rational recognition of an intelligence that does not base itself on the too orderly working of reason and intellect. We are afraid to rely on the spontaneous functioning with which we are naturally endowed, but which gets blocked when restrained in its natural working by efforts to understand it through conventional techniques.

While spontaneous activity might seem unusual to the average person, it is the normal procedure for the man of wisdom. His success is actually due mostly to a sense of confidence that arises through a lack of self-frustrating anxiety. At the same time, he is perfectly capable, by the same token, of doing something that comes naturally in the prevailing circumstances without undue regard to convention. His actions seem unpredictable precisely because they are natural and spontaneous.

30. Seekers who are using their minds to seek Mind, paying far too much attention to what others say, hoping to reach the goal through mere learning, are inviting frustration. Some of the ancients, called 'sages', who were able to abandon learning and come to rest in spontaneity, had sharp minds, and hastened to discard all learning as soon as they heard the Doctrine proclaimed.

These days people seem inclined only to stuff themselves with conceptual deductions, and to seek book-knowledge everywhere, calling this 'Dharma-practice'. They do not realise that more and more conceptual deductions only pile up obstacles and lead to indigestion. When knowledge and concepts are not digested, they become poisons – they belong only to the plane of samsara, totally absent in the Absolute.

So it is said, "In the armory of the sovereign, there is no sword of Thusness." In the Void of the Womb of Tathagatas, dualism does not exist because the smallest hairbreadth of anything cannot exist there. It is for this reason that the Buddha said, "When I was with Dipamkara Buddha there was not a particle of anything for me to attain."

Only he can become a perfectly tranquil man who totally gives up empiricism and does not rely upon any sense-based knowledge and deductions. There is no unalterable Dharma which the Tathagata could have preached. Just put all mental activity to rest and achieve tranquillity. Do not regard as an immutable concept any particular teaching suited to a certain occasion. The canonical teachings of the Three Vehicles are just remedies for temporary needs, and differ from one another. It is stupid to begin by thinking things out and end up in confusion.

The specific area of enormous confusion is: What does Self-realisation mean, and what is Self-realisation supposed to do for the seeker – what will he get that he did not have earlier?

Conditioned as they are by hundreds of years of confusion, the spiritual seekers have come to have the idea that the Self-realised sage is a kind of superman, a 'perfect' human being, totally disciplined, totally in control of his body and mind, whom everyone looks up to for advice and guidance in daily living, and who has the power to protect his disciples from all. And, of course, there are plenty of people who do not fail to take full advantage of this fact. Hence, so many prosperous ashrams and millionaire gurus.

Thus, the area of confusion for most spiritual seekers is around two questions:

a) What precisely is Self-realisation?

b) What do I expect Self-realisation to do for me for the rest of my life that I did not have before?

It is strange that in all the books I have read about the talks between a Guru and his disciples, I have never come across these specific questions being asked or answered! It is actually the great Buddha who has given specific answers to these vital questions:

a) Enlightenment means the *total* acceptance of the fact: Events happen, deeds are done, consequences happen, but there is no individual doer of any deed.

b) Enlightenment means the end of suffering. 'Suffering' in this sense obviously cannot mean the pain in the moment, as an interdependent counterpart of pleasure in the moment, which depends upon the destiny of the person concerned. Obviously the Buddha uses the word 'suffering' for the unhappiness that the human being has created for himself because of his mistaken belief in his own volition, free will, his responsibility for his own actions – the load of guilt and shame for his own actions and a heavier load of hatred and malice towards the 'other' for his actions. The end of the suffering is the disappearance of this load of hatred.

There is another area of confusion where some seekers have had a spiritual experience of 'oneness and ecstasy'. What these people forget is that the experience was in the moment, a free sample, a gift from God; that does not make them God's favourites. It was a gratuitous proof that the separate entity was an illusion and that Reality is Oneness. When this fact is forgotten, what happens is the possibility that thereafter the seeker concerned seeks a repetition of that experience and not the Ultimate Understanding. He forgets that the experience was a happening over which he had no control, and tries all kinds of methods and disciplines in order to 'achieve' more experiences.

What the seeker has to remember is that what is necessary is to be in that mental state of total relaxation, with the total absence of all conceptualising, in which the vacant mind would be able to *receive* the happening called 'enlightenment', which really is an impersonal phenomenon.

Unfortunately, the traditional approach is from the periphery inwards through time, practice, discipline and renunciation, gradually coming upon that inner beauty – in fact to make oneself narrow, petty and shoddy. Peal off little by little, take time, tomorrow will do, next life will do, but where does that take the seeker? Nothing but frustration, because the mind has been made dull, insensitive, incapable of receiving the Final Understanding. What is really necessary is a total revolution, a complete mutation in our minds, in our daily living. What is necessary is the total acceptance that everything is a happening according to God's Will or the Cosmic Law, and not the doing by any autonomous individual entity and, therefore, any rivalry with the 'other' is sheer stupidity.

The basic problem, therefore, is the sense of personal doership in the 'me'. How does the 'me' arise? A psychologist, A. Gesele, has observed the development of the self in children at various stages in the early years of life.

He says:

"Up to eighteen months of age, the child is self-engrossed but not self-aware, since he does not very clearly realise the 'not-self'. At two years, he begins to use self-reference words, 'me', 'you', 'mine', 'I' in that order. At three years of age, the idea of 'persons' becomes clear. At five and six, the child begins to see even in terms of individual qualities."

It is this 'self', this separative, self-centred activity which imagines that one day it will make itself something that it is not. What is to be understood is that there is no 'becoming' of the self; there can only *happen* the ending of selfishness, of anxiety, of sorrow, which are the contents of the psyche, the 'me'. There can only be the ending of all that, and most importantly, *such ending is not a matter of duration*. It is actually a matter of apperceiving that there never was a 'me' as the doer of any deed, and such apperception is a happening in the moment, never in duration.

It is an interesting fact that sorrow, memory, the thought of 'me', all belong to time, and when one stays in the present moment – for instance, when one is attending to something with the working mind totally engrossed in what is being done, something extraordinarily pure and beautiful happens: the 'me' is absent. In fact the 'me' – even as mere identification with name and form – exists only in relationship with the 'other'. When the 'me' – the seeker – is absent, there can never be any confusion: the 'me' as the seeker-doer is the confusion. Absence of conceptualising is all that is necessary for the Final Understanding.

31. There is a question from the seeker: "You say 'Mind is the Buddha', but which is the mind that is the Buddha – the ordinary mind or the Enlightened mind? In the teaching of the Three Vehicles it is stated that both exist. Why do you deny it?"

The Master gives an answer:

"In the teaching of the Three Vehicles, it is clearly stated that both the ordinary and Enlightened minds are illusions. All this clinging to the idea of existing things, which are illusory, hides Mind from you. When Bodhidharma came from the West, he clearly pointed out that the substance of which all men are composed is the Buddha. What you people do is to hold on to concepts such as 'ordinary' and 'Enlightened', building up thoughts outward where they gallop about like horses.

Therefore, I tell you Mind is the Buddha. As soon as conceptualising begins, you fall into dualism. Beginningless time and the present moment are the same – no this and no that. Total acceptance of this truth is called complete and unexcelled Enlightenment."

The seeker asks for a clarification on what the Master said about beginningless time and the present being the same.

The Master explains that it is the seeker's seeking itself which makes a difference between them. Those categories have no real existence. So if 'mind' is not really 'Mind', and as all categories are illusions, where can the seeker hope to find anything?

We abolish opposing positions in space by stating that noumenally there is neither 'here' nor 'there'; we abolish opposing positions in time by stating that there is neither 'now' nor 'then'; we abolish opposing positions of 'me' and the 'other' by stating that there is neither 'this' nor 'that'. All the three statements between them abolish opposing positions of the thinker in both space and time. But the problem is that the thinking entity, as such, remains intact. There continues to be a 'who' that has been removed from space, time and subject-object identification. Thus, while their relative positions have been removed, space-time-thinker all continue to exist as underlying concepts, and until these remaining objects are further negated, the entity 'me' remains intact.

What needs to be apperceived is the basic and fundamental fact that 'space-time' itself is a mere concept that enables noumenal manifestation to happen and, therefore, most importantly, 'I' – which is all that 'we' could all possibly be, as *'we' are Infinity and Intemporality* – to become aware of Itself. Apperceiving this is the Ultimate Understanding. The fact that 'we' seem to experience the contrasting elements like pleasure and pain is the inevitable effect of 'duality', the very basis of the manifestation and its functioning that we call daily living. The duality exists in every conceivable element, beginning with male and female.

In other words, space-time is nothing independent to which we are bound, but only a mechanical extension that renders us objectively perceptible to subjective perceiving. *Since we are all objects, the perceiving must necessarily be in a totally different dimension of pure Subjectivity.*

The very basis of enlightenment is the cessation of 'thinking', of conceptualising, and it is of the utmost importance to realise that there cannot be any prescriptive method to bring it about, for the simple reason that any such effort could only emanate from a 'me' that is itself nothing but a concept. In other words, so long as there is a phenomenal 'me' making an effort, the noumenal 'I' cannot enter – the situation is not vacant!

32. The student complains that the Master has not taught the disciples how to get rid of illusion.

The Master explains that *both the arising of illusion and the elimination of illusion are illusory.*

Illusion is not something *rooted* in Reality; it exists merely because of dualistic thinking in opposite concepts like 'ordinary' and 'Enlightened'. If this conceptualising ceases, there will not be even a hairbreadth of anything left on which to lay hold. This is the meaning of "letting go with both hands," for then you will certainly discover the Buddha in your Mind.

The student questions: "If there is nothing on which to lay hold, and if Mind is used for transmission, how can you say that Mind too does not exist?"

The answer is that *no Dharma whatever can be called transmission. The understanding of this Mind implies no Mind and no Dharma.*

The question remains: If there is no Mind and no Dharma, what is meant by the transmission?

The answer is that it is because of this apparent problem that Bodhidharma said:

"The nature of the Mind when understood,
No human speech can compass or disclose,
Enlightenment is naught to be attained,
And he that gains it does not say he knows."

The Master added: "If I were to make this clear to you, I doubt if you could stand up to it."

The very first thought is the arising of Consciousness – I AM – and this thought is impersonal, direct and immediate – there is no question of ignorance or knowledge. It is the objectivisation of what-we-ARE. This kind of impersonal thought makes for living without identification with any separate entity-doer.

The other kind of thought – thinking, conceptualising – arises after Consciousness becomes identified with a particular form as a separate, suppositionally subjective entity; it is with this entity that questions arise about bondage and liberation, ignorance and knowledge. Any thinking proceeding through the intermediary of such an entity objectivises everything all the time, because that is its nature and function. Such thinking can only create bondage because it means the separation of 'self' and the 'other', which is the basis of ignorance and knowledge. Once the thinking as an individual doer-entity ceases, objectivisation also ceases.

Knowledge, as the interrelated opposite of ignorance, is in the realm of temporal conceptualising, whereas knowing is direct, intuitive, without the intermediacy of thinking. When a person knows, he does not have to ask himself whether he is right or wrong, the interdependent contraries. A man never has to say "I think I am alive and present here." He *knows*. But it is possible for a clever person to argue with a simple man and confuse him so much at the intellectual level that the simple man who 'knows' may be persuaded to think he does not know.

The distinction between knowledge and knowing, it must be repeated, may be subtle but is very significant. When knowing *happens* there is freedom from the bondage of knowledge. Knowledge, based on pride, can only pretend to know.

33. The Master was trying to explain to the seeker that what he had been trying to do was to see Reality in the objective world, when whatever he saw could only be a reflection of Reality, or Mind. He said, "You would be like a man looking at his face in the mirror; however clearly you saw your features, it would still be a reflection. So long as you are concerned with some means like doctrines, you will never understand Mind. What you should do is to listen to those who tell you to open wide both your hands as if you had nothing to lose. If even solid things do not exist, what use can you make of reflections? The Ultimate Understanding can happen only when all seeking ceases. Mind is only one and there is no doctrine which can be put into words."

The essence of Advaita is the fact that what-we-ARE cannot be comprehended, because if there were a comprehender (other than what-we-ARE) to comprehend what-we-ARE, that comprehender would become an object to be comprehended by another comprehender and so on. In other words, what-we-ARE phenomenally is conceptual, what-we-ARE non-conceptually is non-conceptuality itself. Therefore, not-knowing – like knowing – is pure Subjectivity. When I wake up, I can only say "I do not know" about something that happened when I was asleep. Both the knowledge in the waking state and the non-knowledge in the sleeping state are phenomenal concepts, but the *Knowingness* – positive or negative – is subjective or noumenal.

What is necessary for the transformation – *para-vritti* – to *happen* is the apprehension by the seeker of his own utter non-existence as an autonomous entity. This apprehension can reveal the noumenal Immensity – the Infinite Intemporality – that we are. But obviously this is beyond the 'word' to accomplish because using words would only be conceptualising in phenomenal duality. The word can only be a pointer; all that the word can do is to remove the conditioning brought about by itself through various concepts, theories and doctrines.

34. To a question by the seeker, "What is meant by relative truth?" (literally "worldly truth"), the Master explains:

"Why are you wasting your time on useless concepts like that?"

Reality is perfect purity, and to be without any concepts at all is called the 'Wisdom of Dispassion'. Whatever you may be doing in your daily living, remain detached from all phenomena; whether you blink an eye or say something, do it with total dispassion, without being involved.

To put it simply, let each thought go as though it were nothing, or let it turn into any natural action. You must get away from the doctrines of existence and non-existence, for Mind is like the sun, forever in the phenomenal Void, shining without wanting to shine.

You will be acting in accordance with the saying "Develop a mind which rests on nothing whatever" (Diamond Sutra), when you are able to cling to nothing whatever (not getting involved). All your most painful practice and efforts will be wasted, along with the most profound knowledge, if you cannot understand this simple truth.

What advantage will you gain by this sort of practice and discipline? As Chih Kung (a famous 6th cent. monk) said, "The Buddha is really the creation of your own mind. How then can he be sought through scriptures?" All your studies will only make you balance yourself between 'ordinary' and 'Enlightened'. Not to see that all methods of following the Way are *ephemeral* is samsaric Dharma:

"Its strength once spent, the arrow falls to earth;
You build up lives which won't fulfil your hopes.
How far below the Transcendental Gate
From which one leap will gain the Buddha's realm."

('Song of Enlightenment' by 7th cent. monk Yung Chia)

Chih Kung also said, "If you do not meet a transcendental teacher, you will have swallowed the Mahayana medicine in vain."

As the sage Jnaneshwar has put it, after completing the book *Anubhavamrita*:

a) O my beloved Guru, this supreme joy of Self-realisation which you have handed to me almost on a platter, I should have liked to enjoy in peace and quiet by myself (but obviously you wish that I should share it with the rest of the world).

b) The Almighty gave the reins of the Light in the hands of the sun, but it is the world that has benefited by this light.

c) That coolness with which the moon has been endowed is beneficial to the trees and vegetation; the water with which the seas have endowed the clouds is for the whole world.

d) The light of the lamp lights up the whole house; the space under the sky is used for the manifestation of the entire universe.

e) Similarly, the power that brings about the operation of tides in the sea is not of the sea but that of the moon; whatever the vernal season brings about is for the benefit of the trees.

f) In the same way, this book is a token of your immense power, O my beloved Guru; otherwise I as such have no independent authority of existence (to write such a book).

g) Also, why should I (after receiving the mighty gift of Unicity) claim any credit for the book and thereby be in the bondage of duality?

h) And then, of course, noumenal Unicity is eternally present in its shining glory and does not need any exegesics (on my part or any one else's).

i) And if I had kept my silence and not said anything on the subject, would the phenomenal manifestation not have been manifested?

j) When manifestation is perceived as an object by another object (posing as the subject) in duality, the perceiver is the perceived; this is the truth which needs no proof.

k) This is the final truth: the identity of the noumenon and the phenomena, the perceiver and the perceived. And the truth did not need this sort of telling (as in this book).

l) If this is so, then what is the point in writing this book? The answer is that the contents of the book are a spontaneous outpouring of the love which the final truth is (I did not write the book!).

m) The favourite subject may be the same, but a new taste and fresh enjoyment is to be had whenever it is discussed afresh.

n) It is for this reason that I have spoken on this subject. It is not as if I have discovered something that was hidden. THAT-which-is is Self-effulgent and in fact, cannot be hidden.

o) All there is, is 'I' – I am the potential plenum and *I can neither hide myself nor show myself.*

35. If you would spend your time learning to halt the concept-forming activities of your mind, you could be sure of ultimately attaining the goal. But you feel obliged to employ your mind 'studying dhyana' or something like that. So it is said that all that the Tathagata taught was just to convert people; it was like pretending yellow leaves are real gold to stop the tears of a child.

What is called supreme perfect wisdom implies that there is really nothing whatever to be attained. You must see clearly that there really is nothing at all – no humans and no Buddhas.

The whole point is that enlightenment is only an impersonal happening: seeing the whole as Reality; no 'one' can get enlightened.

36. The sixth Patriarch told the Elder Wei Ming: "Perhaps you will concentrate your thoughts for a moment and avoid thinking in terms of good and evil." Ming did as he was told, and the sixth Patriarch continued, "While you are not thinking of good or evil, just at this very moment, return to what you were before your parents were born." Even as the words were spoken, Ming arrived at a certain tacit understanding.

The Ultimate Understanding is:

a) That there is only ONE Source, pure Subjectivity, by whatever name known: Noumenon, Absolute, Consciousness, Primal Energy, or, as the common man would prefer, God.

b) That the phenomenal manifestation is an emanation of, or the reflection of, the ONE Source, consisting of thousands of species of three-dimensional objects, extended in space-time.

c) That, therefore, the human being is one of the species of three-dimensional objects: a sentient object, with the different senses, through which the functioning of the phenomenal manifestation happens – what we know as daily living.

d) That 'life' as we know it, in the functioning of the manifestation, happens because the primal energy, functioning through the billions of human beings, produces through each one of them, every instant, whatever is supposed to be produced according to a conceptual Cosmic Law that has prevailed since the beginning of time, the basis of which the human being, a three-dimensional object, could not possibly imagine, let alone 'Know'.

e) That the human being is essentially a uniquely programmed instrument (genes with unique DNA, plus the environmental conditioning which every human being receives at home, in society, in school, in church or temple) – a programming over which the human instrument could not possibly have had any control.

f) That the very basis of the phenomenal manifestation is the existence of interconnected opposites of every conceivable variety, beginning with male and female, beautiful and ugly, good and bad, and everything else.

g) That the very basis of life as we know it, is the constant choosing by the human being between the many interconnected opposites and, therefore, being happy or unhappy. Thus, this comparing and choosing and judging is the basic cause of human suffering.

h) That this comparison and choice cannot be made by the inert three-dimensional object, and so, the Source had to create an apparent doer of the actions – the ego – by divine hypnosis (a thought which identifies the ego with a particular body-mind organism and a name, and creates a separate entity *with a sense of personal doership*).

i) That the basis of the human suffering is the sense of personal doership; this creates the load of guilt and shame, and also pride and arrogance for one's own actions, and another heavier load of hatred for the 'others' for their actions which have harmed one in some way.

j) That it is the ego, a mere thought created by divine hypnosis, that causes the human being to consider himself an independent, autonomous entity responsible for his actions, who is in bondage and who is seeking freedom from that bondage.

k) That the only way to remove this monstrous load on the mind is to accept *totally* what the Buddha has put so succinctly and so powerfully:

   "Events happen, deeds are done, consequences happen, but there is no individual doer of any deed."

l) It is obvious that since one is not the doer, there is nothing really that one can do to accept totally that he is not the doer. It can only happen, like any other happening, if it is God's Will/Cosmic Law.

m) What the human being can do is, with sincerity and humility, to investigate thoroughly any action he is particularly sure is his action. In every single case, without exception, he will keep on coming to the conclusion that the action simply could not have been 'his' action. If a particular thought had not *happened*, his action would not have happened, and he had no control over the happening of that thought. Or, if he had not *happened* to be at a particular place at a particular time, and *happened* to see something, or hear something, or smell something, or taste something, or touch something, the action would not have happened. Each time, his intellectual acceptance goes deeper and deeper, and at some point of time, depending on his destiny, God's Will/Cosmic Law, a divine flash of total acceptance is likely to happen: "I simply cannot be the doer of any action; no one can."

Advaita on Tao
Comments on Lao Tzu

The Book of the Way

Preface

The Book of the Way, or *Tao Te Ching*, is said to have been written by the great Chinese sage Lao Tzu while on his way to the mountains, where he is said to have disappeared into immortality. Legend has it that the guard of the kingdom stopped him, and only agreed to let him pass if he wrote down his knowledge of 'The Way' first, for the benefit of all those remaining behind in society. The result was a small book of 81 short verses expressing the essence of 'The Tao'.

2500 years later, though showing no signs of heading for the mountains even at the ripe old age of 90, the great Indian Advaita Master Ramesh S. Balsekar has written his own short *Book of the Way*. Inspired by the original *Tao Te Ching*, these 90 verses express the essence of Advaita Vedanta, while bringing out the 'sameness' at the core of these two great traditions. Although this work has the flavour of the *Tao Te Ching* interwoven throughout its pages, rather than being a mere commentary it is in fact an original work that stands on its own merits.

Perhaps if Lao Tzu had been a master of Advaita instead of Taoism, his *Book of the Way* might have looked something like this...

INTRODUCTION
BY RAMESH BALSEKAR

Who is Lao Tzu?

Lao Tzu is supposed to have lived in China 500 years before Christ, a contemporary of the Buddha and Confucius. According to legend, having become disenchanted with the prevailing rules and regulations, he decided to leave the country and find a place where he could live naturally and peacefully. When he reached the pass in the mountains, 'the keeper of the pass' wanted to know who he was and where he was going. The simple man was so impressed by what Lao Tzu told him, that he persuaded Lao Tzu to stay for a few days and write down his understanding of daily life. What resulted is now known as the *Tao Te Ching*, which is considered as one of the great spiritual classics of all time.

The following writing was inspired by my readings of the *Tao Te Ching*. The source of my information is mainly the free flowing rendition of Stephen Mitchell, and, more so, the recently produced book by Colin D. Mallard, Ph.D., which I found extremely useful.

1. The Source dreams, and the manifestation comes into being – mystery.

   MAYA – based on duality, beginning with male and female, and duality of every conceivable kind.

   The manifest and the Unmanifest are not two.

ॐ

2. According to the basic duality in manifestation, beginning with male and female, ugliness comes into being as soon as something is labelled as 'beautiful'.

Being and Non-Being arise together; and so do long and short, difficult and easy, high and low, sound and silence, before and after, pleasure and pain. These are complementary opposites: one cannot exist without the other. That is the nature of daily living, but let us not forget that there can always be the 'middle' that is neither.

The wise man lives his life never forgetful of this basic fact of life – merely witnessing life as it happens without judging anyone.

ॐ

3. Let us admire the work, not the object through which it happens; otherwise, when the gifted are admired and praised, the ordinary people feel inadequate.

When one possesses more than one needs, should not some of it be used for the benefit of the society?

ॐ

4. The Source, the Void, is eternal and filled with infinite possibilities – good, bad and indifferent.

It is like a well, used but never emptied.

ॐ

5. To the sage, life is like a dream and everything manifested is an illusion, including all the human characters which live in this dream, dreamed by the Source.

When one suddenly comes across a magnificent scene like the Himalayan mountains, all there is is powerful Impersonal Awareness in the moment; when identified consciousness arises again, possessiveness makes us want a photograph immediately, and a magnificent painting in due course.

ॐ

6. Everything in the manifestation – and its functioning that we call 'life' – is a natural expression of the Unmanifest Source.

What should the human being do, with the same spontaneity, other than merely witnessing whatever happens, without spoiling the naturalness of it by comparing and judging?

ॐ

7. What can the present moment be other than the Eternal and Infinite?

The 'present moment' was never born and cannot die.

ॐ

8. The Ultimate Understanding – the goal and the path – is like flowing water, flowing to the lower places, nourishing all things on the way, without effort.

The Ultimate Understanding can only happen. It cannot be achieved by effort.

ॐ

9. When one works essentially with the expectation of getting money and security, one invites frustration in case of failure.

Disaster soon follows the flaunting of wealth and power: the next generation comes to grief.

Pursuing the approval of others means becoming their prisoner.

Doing whatever seems necessary without undue expectation, and accepting whatever happens, brings peace of mind.

ॐ

10. In the absence of unnecessary conceptualising and objectivising, the mind retains its natural vacancy and is in contact with the Source.

When the inner vision is clear, and the whole is seen as a whole and not a collection of parts, harmony and peace of mind prevails.

ॐ

11. It is a strange fact of life that what one sees as the obvious is the wheel and the spokes, but it is the hole in the middle which allows the wheel to turn.

What is useful in a clay pot? It is the emptiness that is used.

We admire the house built by bricks and wood and steel, but it is the emptiness inside where people live. It is as openings that doors and windows are useful.

Being can only come out of Non-Being.

12. Everything in the world is a happening according to God's Will or the Cosmic Law. Why react to what the society considers honour or disgrace? Why not give up self-importance and accept disgrace? The basis of life is pleasure or pain from moment to moment, over which we have no control.

When life is accepted precisely the way it happens, there is peace and harmony.

ॐ

13. Look for the Source, and It cannot be seen; nor can It be heard. There is no brightness above It and no darkness below It.

It is the ever-pregnant Silence.

Formless Itself, It contains all forms. There is no beginning to approach and no end to reach.

We cannot know It because It is what we are.

There is neither Beingness nor Non-Beingness.

This is Wisdom.

14. One can only attempt to describe the man of wisdom and understanding.

He is generally as careful as a man crossing an icy stream, as alert as a warrior crossing enemy lines, as courteous as a visiting guest, as fluid as melting ice, as malleable as a carver's material, as receptive as a valley, as transparent as clear water.

He is as natural and spontaneous as can be.

ॐ

15. The wise man does not seek anything or pursue anything; he thoroughly enjoys whatever comes his way.

In any situation, he does precisely what he feels he should do as if he has total free will; but accepting that no one has had any control over the results and consequences of their actions, he sits back, relaxes, and witnesses whatever happens, without condemning anyone for anything, without any regrets about the past, without any complaints in the present, without any expectations in the future.

In a way, he is, in practice, the ever-present Consciousness Itself.

16. As soon as an ego is created through identification with a particular body-mind organism, the ego is connected to the Source, the Impersonal Consciousness, as identified consciousness. This connection continues until the death of the body, and then, since the ego is no longer required, the identified consciousness again becomes the Impersonal Consciousness as the Source.

The sage, living his life without the sense of personal doership, never gets involved in daily living and, therefore, finds his connection with the Source never broken. He lives in peace and harmony until, when death happens, the consciousness returns to the Source.

ॐ

17. When the leader is a wise man, the people hardly realise the existence of the leader; when the leader is aware of his being a leader, and governs with moderation, he is loved; then comes the leader who is feared, and finally the leader who is despised.

The wise leader says little, and when the work is finished, the people think they did it themselves.

True leadership consists in doing whatever is necessary without the pride of being a leader.

18. When the Source is forgotten, goodness and morality appear;

When goodness and morality appear, vanity and hypocrisy are born;

When peace and harmony are absent in the family, family values are espoused;

When a country falls into chaos, patriots are born.

If everyone lived with self-esteem, there would be no need for rules and regulations in life.

19. When concepts of morality and justice are forgotten, people spontaneously do what is natural; if the idea of profit could disappear, theft would come to an end.

What is needed for happy living is a personal religion based on self-esteem and universal brotherhood, based on non-doership: *Thy Will Be Done, O Lord!*

ॐ

20. Most of our unhappiness is caused by comparison with one's peers and conceptualising about what might happen in the illusory future.

Something always happens. Why worry unnecessarily? Worrying has not done anything for anyone.

Why keep pursuing a preference and remain frustrated? Why not enjoy the variety of life?

It has been everyone's experience in life that there has often been great pleasure at the end of pain.

21. The mystery of life proves to be no mystery after all.

The Unicity of the Source has become the basic duality of the manifestation (and its functioning that we call 'life'), beginning with male and female – duality of every conceivable kind.

Therefore, in life, we have to have wealth and poverty, saints and psychopaths, healthy children and handicapped children.

All there really IS, is the Absolute Reality.

There is no creation, only an appearance in Consciousness, which disappears and appears again.

ॐ

22. Rigidity in life can be fatal. What is needed is supple adaptability.

The basis of happiness in life is not to pursue a preference, and not to have any expectations in the future. This means the total acceptance that nothing can happen unless that is the Will of God – the Cosmic Law, the basis of which it is impossible for the human being to know because it is too vast and too complex.

Yield to the Will of God, and do whatever you need to do in any given situation. Then there will be no pride, no guilt, no hatred. This means happiness through peace and harmony – *Sukha-Shanti.*

ॐ

23. The wise man speaks and acts only when necessary, and this he does with compassion and without any expectation.

He accepts that the basis of daily living is that there will be pleasure one moment, and pain in the next moment. Even in nature, fierce winds last only for a day or two.

Having accepted totally that "Thou art the doer and Thou art the experiencer," life becomes spontaneous and carefree.

ॐ

24. The wise man does whatever he is doing because he loves to do it, not because he is forced to do it.

He does it without any expectation and, therefore, there is neither pride nor guilt, nor disappointment.

This means peace of mind.

ॐ

25. The Source, eternally present, may be seen as potential Energy, activising Itself in endless cycles: manifestation and non-manifestation, the presence and absence of the universe.

The man of wisdom sees this as MAYA, and does not take anything that happens in life too seriously. Therefore, there is peace and harmony.

ॐ

26. The root of light is Nothingness;

The source of all movement is stillness;

The source of all sound is silence.

ॐ

27. The wise man is always alert and watchful when he moves about and is totally relaxed when he is home.

He witnesses whatever happens not as anyone's doing but as a happening that is supposed to happen precisely as it has happened. He, therefore, never condemns anyone for anything – neither himself nor the 'other'.

He enjoys himself thoroughly when his preferences are satisfied, but never pursues any preference; he is, therefore, never frustrated.

28. Life lived senselessly and frivolously can only end in disaster. Restlessness prevents the happening of peace of mind.

ॐ

29. The man of wisdom lives in harmony with nature, and in harmonious relationship with the 'other'.

He is not interested in leaving his mark when he dies.

He is always available to others for guidance but does not offer it frivolously.

Awakening cannot happen in the absence of an appropriate relationship between the Guru and the disciple.

ॐ

30. Happiness through peace of mind – *Sukha-Shanti* – cannot happen unless there is total understanding and acceptance of the basic duality in every walk of life, otherwise there would be judgement and blame, almost all the time, based on preferences.

If there is total understanding and acceptance of the basic duality, then there is humility and a total absence of condemning anyone for anything – neither oneself nor the 'other'. What exists is only impersonal witnessing of life's happenings without any judging.

ॐ

31. The man of wisdom witnesses the manifest universe emerging from the Unmanifest Source, with its inherent beauty based on duality, and accepts whatever is as precisely what is supposed to be in every detail.

ॐ

32. The world, as it has emerged from the Unmanifest Void, is precisely as it is supposed to be. How can any man expect to improve it in any way?

Duality is the very basis of the manifestation and its functioning that we call 'living'. If it is not totally accepted, we continuously ask questions like, "Why does God create handicapped children?" and we invite frustration and unhappiness.

ॐ

33. It is a fact of life that violence, even with justification, rebounds on itself. Where armies have passed, the earth is torn and soaked in blood.

The man of wisdom knows that whatever he has done, and whatever anyone else has done, was precisely what was supposed to happen according to the Cosmic Law. He goes along with the flow of life.

ॐ

34. The wise ones enter a battle only when compelled to do so, and then with restraint and compassion, never rejoicing in victory or revenge.

ॐ

35. The Absolute Nothingness that is the source of all forms cannot be defined. From It untold galaxies emerge, and into It they dissolve.

If only people would accept the 'what-is' as it is, there would be peace and harmony in the world.

ॐ

36. It is conceptualising and objectivising which creates distinctions and comparisons between things, and creates conflict.

Wise people stay clear of judgements, accepting that everything happens according to the Cosmic Law.

And then, suddenly, the phenomenal manifestation could disappear into the Nothingness as if there never was a creation.

ॐ

37. To know others and deal with others requires intelligence; to know oneself and deal with oneself needs wisdom.

Prestige, power and possessions may for most people represent wealth. But such wealth does not equal the satisfaction which someone has, who is content with what he has. The two cannot be compared.

To accept life as it happens means being ready to accept death whenever it may happen, as part of living.

ॐ

38. Life has been happening from time immemorial like a flow according to the Cosmic Law of Nature.

The sage accepts whatever comes his way as part of the natural flow of life, content and happy with 'what-is', because he has been wise enough never to have pursued either his preference or any other pleasure.

ॐ

39. Those who have a harmonious relationship with others – whoever they may be – exude a peacefulness that defies description, and which attracts people towards them.

They cannot explain, when asked, what makes them so transparently happy. They are asked what they have done to be so peaceful, and they can only confess that they have not done anything particularly different. The fact of the matter is that they have been naturally able to accept that nothing can happen unless it is the Will of God, and that truly no individual entity can be the doer of any deed, good or bad.

It is a tragic joke that this is the basis of every religion: *Thy Will Be Done.*

40. It is a basic mistake to seek the Source, to be one with God.

The Source is all there is – either as the Unmanifest or the entire manifest universe. Who is to seek the Source?

When this is deeply apperceived the seeker gets absorbed in that apperception, and lives his life never again considering himself or any other individual as the doer of any action, good or bad.

ॐ

41. Enlightenment means, in simple words, seeing things as they are: the phenomenal expression of the unmanifest noumenal Source.

There is no individual entity, really, to be strong or weak, wise or ignorant – only a human instrument through which life happens according to the Cosmic Law.

Exhibiting one's strength and power means inviting challenge and conflict.

ॐ

42. The man of wisdom, going with the flow of life, appears to be doing nothing, and yet nothing remains undone.

The only way to live is to let life flow and be in harmony with the 'other', whoever he may be, with the understanding that nothing can happen unless it is the Will of God, or the Cosmic Law.

Daily living means doing whatever needs to be done, without any expectations in the future.

To see the simplicity of life is to be in harmony with It, the Source, with the connection never being broken.

43. The man of wisdom happens to be wise without having made any effort to be wise. Whatever he does, he does *as if* he is doing it, and nothing remains undone. Free of the illusion of personal doership, accepting everything as the Will of God, he lives in peace and harmony without considering anyone as his enemy.

When natural spontaneity is lost, there arises the concept of goodness; when goodness is lost, there arises the concept of morality; when morality is lost, there comes ritual, and that is the beginning of chaos.

44. It appears as if one man speaks and another listens; but, if neither were conscious, or if they were in deep sleep or under sedation, neither would be able to speak or listen, or do anything else.

It is therefore clear that it is the Impersonal Consciousness, as the Source, which brings about the speaking through one human instrument and the listening through another human instrument.

Total apperception of this simple fact means enlightenment.

45. When leaders are in illusion, there is turmoil and life becomes uncertain. At this time, an awakened leader comes along and works with total humility, and with the understanding that it is the Source which brings about whatever is supposed to happen, through whichever person it is supposed to happen. The society, of course, will necessarily consider each happening as someone's action, and deal with it appropriately according to the prevailing social regulations and legal provisions.

With the sense of personal doership totally uprooted from the ego, the wise leader lives an unpretentious life, not polished like fine jade, but rugged and simple as a stone.

ॐ

46. The human being is a three-dimensional object in the totality of manifestation – the Being that has emerged from Non-Being, the manifest that has emerged from the Unmanifest Source.

ॐ

47. The man of wisdom hears of Advaita and at once becomes its embodiment; the ordinary man hears of Advaita and is in two minds; a foolish man hears about Advaita and bursts out laughing.

Thus it is that in daily living, the path home seems to be leading away from home, the short-cut seems too long, real strength appears weak, the easy way appears difficult, real happiness seems empty, true clarity seems obscure, genuine beauty goes unnoticed, the greatest love seems indifferent, and the greatest wisdom appears foolish.

It is a strange fact of life that one seeks the Source, or God, when it so happens that THAT Source is all there is, anywhere and everywhere.

48. The basis of the phenomenal manifestation – which has emerged from the Source, the noumenal Unicity – and its functioning that we know as living is duality, beginning with male and female, and including duality of every conceivable kind.

When this basic duality of life is totally accepted – that a saint cannot exist without a psychopath – peace and harmony prevail naturally.

ॐ

49. Ever since a baby is born and seeks its mother's breast intuitively, the purpose and meaning of life would seem to be the seeking of 'happiness'. For the new-born baby it is the mother's milk; thereafter the meaning of 'happiness' keeps changing until the adult human being pursues pleasure in life as happiness, and this pursuit ends in frustration.

It is only the man of wisdom who realises that true happiness lies in a harmonious relationship with the 'other', whoever it may be. The basis of this relationship which brings the required happiness is the total acceptance that everything is a happening according to God's Will – the Cosmic Law – and not the deed of a human being. Such acceptance ends the load of suffering that man was carrying in the form of hatred for himself for his actions and a bigger load of hatred towards others for their actions.

ॐ

50. The sage knows that every action is in fact a happening according to God's Will – the Cosmic Law.

This means doing whatever needs to be done without having any expectation.

The way the sage lives is itself the teaching he gives; teaching through action, not words.

ॐ

51. The man of wisdom prefers peace of mind – *Sukha-Shanti* – to fame, contentment to wealth.

He is indifferent to success or failure, and is content with whatever happens in life.

He does not pursue anything particular in life.

52. The man of wisdom is he who lets life flow, accepting whatever comes to him, never pursuing anything.

He is prisoner of nothing; he is master of the world.

ॐ

53. There is no greater suffering than being attached to something or someone, no greater foolishness than not knowing when one has enough, no greater misfortune than wanting what others have.

The basis of peace of mind is to be content with what one has and thus be in harmony with the world at large.

ॐ

54. The more information one has, the less one seems to understand.

The sage knows that he found Reality when he stopped searching. He accepts life as it happens, witnessing everything as a happening, precisely the way it is supposed to be.

ॐ

55. The pursuit of knowledge leads to more and more being accumulated.

The pursuit of apperception leads to more and more falling away of accumulated concepts.

When the sense of personal doership has been uprooted, there is no question of anything being finished or half-finished.

ॐ

56. Enlightened living means not judging anyone as a good person or a bad person, whatever the society's award may be, concerning any particular action by a particular person. This is based on the total acceptance that the saint had no control over being a saint, nor did the psychopath choose to be a psychopath.

Enlightened living means witnessing the movie of life, including the biological reactions in the body-mind organism from scene to scene, without the ego judging anyone. A particular scene might arouse anger, or disgust, or fear, or compassion, but the ego remains unconcerned with the biological reaction.

ॐ

57. With the sense of personal doership having been totally uprooted from the ego of the sage, the understanding has happened that the ego is merely an instrument through which the Source, the Impersonal Consciousness, functions through the body-mind organism to bring about whatever action is supposed to happen.

Therefore, the sage is no longer attached to any of life's happenings, and the ultimate test of enlightenment is that the sage is not attached to life and is ready to welcome death at any moment.

ॐ

58. The basis of daily living is the interhuman relationships between 'me' and the 'other'. Therefore, the Source, the Impersonal Consciousness, had to identify with each human body-mind organism, and create a separate entity known as the 'ego'.

This ego has to live its life as a separate entity in whatever circumstances it has been placed. As such, each ego is connected to the Source, the Impersonal Consciousness, while daily living takes place.

When the body is dead, there is no more need of a separate entity, the ego; and so Consciousness gives up the individual identification and again remains as the Impersonal Consciousness.

ॐ

59. The Ultimate Understanding is for the ego to realise that fundamentally, each ego can only be the One Reality, the Source – the Impersonal Consciousness identified with each body-mind organism as a separate entity.

Therefore, every ego is, fundamentally, the Impersonal Consciousness. With this basic understanding, interhuman relationships become totally harmonious. Suffering no longer exists in the form of guilt and shame for one's own actions or hatred for the 'other' for his actions. There is a clear sense of universal brotherhood, and peace of mind as the supreme happiness.

60. When witnessing happens of whatever is to be witnessed, without any judgement, the heart is filled with infinite peace, in the total absence of hatred.

This means clearly seeing 'what-is' without the slightest resistance. This saves an enormous amount of energy that would otherwise have been wasted in judging people and condemning them.

This also means remaining connected to the Source all the time without the connection being broken through involvement in daily living.

ॐ

61. Before space-time came into being, along with the phenomenal manifestation, there was only the Source, the Unmanifest Unicity, the potential Energy.

When the potential Energy activised Itself, there suddenly appeared the phenomenal universe functioning in space-time.

62. The Unmanifest Source, the potential Energy, activised Itself into the phenomenal manifestation. For the functioning of this manifestation that we call daily living, the Source, as Consciousness, had to identify Itself with each body-mind organism as a separate entity – ego – with the sense of personal doership.

The ego naturally gets involved in daily living, and thus has to carry the burden of hatred for itself and others for their respective actions. This load disappears with the total understanding that everything happens according to God's Will and that the human being is only an instrument through which actions happen.

This is enlightenment, which means peace of mind. This is too simple for the human mind, which creates a mass of complex concepts, and remains unhappy. Not many are enlightened.

ॐ

63. The total acceptance that everything happens according to Divine Will and that the human being, a mere instrument, is incapable of doing anything, is enlightenment. This results in remaining connected to the Source all the time, without the connection ever being broken. Thus, daily living becomes spontaneous, simple, free.

The wider this understanding spreads, the wider would be the benefits – to the family, to the neighbours, to the nation, to the whole world.

The total understanding brings about a deep happiness through peace and harmony.

ॐ

64. The remarkable vitality of the child is based on the total absence of the sense of personal doership.

He who seeks enlightenment through forced discipline and spiritual practices only invites frustration and exhaustion.

ॐ

65. With the sense of personal doership permanently uprooted from the ego, the sage lives his life unostentatiously, remarkably similar in appearance to that of the ordinary man, but actually the fact of the matter is that his relationships with others are astonishingly smooth and harmonious. He thus experiences the basic, innate harmony of life.

The sage goes through life not pursuing any preference, accepting whatever comes, from moment to moment, without demanding anything, accepting everything including pains and losses, as his destiny.

Being permanently connected to the Source, honour and dishonour have no meaning for him.

66. To become a master of life is truly quite simple: let life flow and do not be attached to anything, not even life itself.

The more clever and ingenious people become, the greater the mischief they get into. The more knowledge they have of laws and regulations, the more effective they become in circumventing them.

Free from desire and totally bereft of the sense of personal doership, the man of wisdom has discovered the innate simplicity of life.

ॐ

67. The sage is totally aware of the basic fact of life: nobody can know what will happen next, disaster can arise from good fortune, and good fortune from disaster.

He lives his life accepting whatever comes from the flow of life.

He is straightforward without being rude. He does not impose himself on others, and people see him as a transparently happy man, totally at peace with himself and in harmony with others.

ॐ

68. The sage does not imprison himself within his own ideas; he is always open to other ideas. He is aware of the secret of life – a tree has to yield to the high winds.

The sage is not imprisoned by the opinions of others, nor by social conventions. He lives with a religion of his own, awakened from the dream.

ॐ

69. When the sage has to govern, he does so with the full understanding that, like frying a fish, when overdone things fall apart.

Centred in the Ultimate Understanding, he governs in such a way that no one is harmed.

ॐ

70. A great nation is aware of the importance of not using force, of the necessity of a softer approach.

When both nations yield, they both get what they need.

ॐ

71. The Ultimate Understanding is beyond intellectual comprehension.

It can only happen through the apperception of the basic truth that the Source is the only Reality.

ॐ

72. The Ultimate Understanding means the total acceptance of 'what-is', including what might appear as a mistake or something half-finished.

ॐ

73. Wisdom consists in:

letting life happen;
giving service without expectation
   of a reward;
savouring that which has no flavour;
giving due attention to the few
   and the insignificant;
reacting to bitterness with kindness
   and to force with softness;
taking adequate care of what seems easy
   before it becomes difficult;
accepting an error promptly
   and rectifying it at once;
seeing things as they are.

ॐ

74. It is a fact of life that:

a) It is necessary to maintain peace and harmony and not let it get lost;

b) It is better to anticipate problems before they happen;

c) Action with expectation means inviting frustration;

d) Unless one is diligent from the very beginning, failure can happen on the verge of success;

e) Wisdom consists in being content with what one has and not continually wanting more and more;

f) It is wisdom to offer advice and guidance only when it is asked for.

ॐ

75. From the beginning of time, no master has been keen to shower his wisdom on others, because most people think they already know both the questions and the answers.

True wisdom understands how life works and how it points to the Oneness from where everything has emerged.

ॐ

76. The sage is revered by people because he competes with no one; he places himself below others and follows them as the shepherd follows the sheep.

When the sage stands before the people, they revere him because they are not intimidated; they know that he has the welfare of everyone at heart.

ॐ

77. The greatness of the sage is not the usual greatness. It lies in being connected to the Source in an unbroken continuity; the usual greatness is petty, insignificant and small.

The sage has three priceless gems:

a) Mercy leading to courage;

b) Frugality leading to generosity;

c) Humility leading to leadership.

This is how the Source takes care of genuine seekers through the sage.

ॐ

78. The successful leader directs his men with smoothness and ease, never placing himself above them, and always being considerate of their needs.

The successful leader remains in the background though he leads people from the front. In victory he is not at all interested in revenge.

Such a man has understood the secret of life, and always acts in accordance with the natural Cosmic Law.

ॐ

79. The successful warrior is aware that underestimating the enemy can be fatal.

He concentrates on his work without wasting time and energy on thinking about what might happen in the future.

ॐ

80. The Ultimate Understanding is so simple, and that is the reason why most people are not really interested.

The sage knows that the ultimate happiness can only be contained in the peace of mind that is found through harmonious relationships with others, and not in the pleasures of life.

His is enlightened living: his clothing is simple, his actions unobtrusive, he is always willing to help others, and his heart is radiant beyond compare.

81. Most people are unable to accept the Ultimate Understanding because it is too simple and cannot accommodate the enormous load of concepts the serious seeker carries in his mind.

ॐ

82. The sage feels no need to stand out.

He does not intrude in people's lives.

He has unburdened himself of all unnecessary conceptualisation, and is always open to whatever the next moment might bring from the Source.

ॐ

83. The basis of daily living is that every individual is forced to live his life in the circumstances in which he has been placed. It is everyone's birthright to exercise his free will in any situation, but he has no control over the result and the consequence of his action. Also, no one has ever known what will happen the next moment: pleasure or pain.

The only way to live one's life is to do whatever one feels like doing and, thereafter, witness whatever happens, without condemning anyone for anything – neither oneself nor the 'other'; to live without any regrets about the past, without any complaints in the present, and without any expectations in the future.

This would be enlightened living.

84. When life becomes intolerable for any reason, people want to give it up. It is not that they welcome death but that they do not want to go on living anymore.

The sage, even in the happiest circumstances, is always ready to welcome death, because he has no attachment to anything, not even life.

ॐ

85. It is a fact of life that the soft, the supple and the yielding are expressions of life; and the stiff, the rigid and the inflexible are expressions of death.

86. Nature is like a drawn bow; as the top lowers, the bottom is raised; as the height diminishes, the width broadens.

In this way, excess and deficiency get perfectly adjusted.

ॐ

87. It is a fact of life that nothing in the world is as soft and yielding as water; and yet nothing can surpass it when it comes to dissolving the hard and the inflexible.

This applies to what happens in daily living. Everyone knows this, but few put this knowledge into practice.

88. The sage always fulfils his obligations and thus has peace of mind, irrespective of what the other party may do. In other words, he does what he would do anyway, irrespective of the result.

This is so because he knows that the result of any action has never, ever been in anyone's control.

ॐ

89. If we find that the residents of a particular society are happy to an unusual extent, there can be only one reason: their relationship with one another is unusually harmonious because they do not compete with one another in the pursuit of pleasure.

Envy and jealousy are, therefore, not present in their interrelationships with one another.

ॐ

90. The man of wisdom has no need to prove any point, nor is he concerned with having the last word.

The more he gives, the more content and happy he is.

The man of wisdom is always found to be a happy and contented man, with no expectations in the future.

ॐ

Publisher's Note

We would like to thank Kirk Andrews and Daniele Legler for their contribution in making this book a possibility. We also thank Dev Varyani and Göran Ekdahl for their continued support in helping us spread the teaching. And, Gary Roba for his invaluable help in editing the book.

OTHER RAMESH BALSEKAR TITLES PUBLISHED BY YOGI IMPRESSIONS

The Ramesh Balsekar Collector's Set (2010)

The End of Duality (2009)

Advaita on Zen and Tao (2008)

90 Steps to Oneness – Wisdom Deck (2007)

The Only Way to Live (2006)

Let Life Flow (2005)

The One in the Mirror (2004)

The Seeking (2004)

The Happening of a Guru: A Biography (2003)

Peace and Harmony in Daily Living (2003)

The Ultimate Understanding (2001)

For information on Ramesh Balsekar, visit:
www.rameshbalsekar.com

For further details, contact:
Yogi Impressions LLP
1711, Centre 1, World Trade Centre,
Cuffe Parade, Mumbai 400 005, India.

Fill in the Mailing List form on our website and receive, via email, information on books, authors, events and more.
Visit: www.yogiimpressions.com

Telephone: (022) 40115981, 22155036
E-mail: yogi@yogiimpressions.com

Join us on Facebook:
www.facebook.com/yogiimpressions

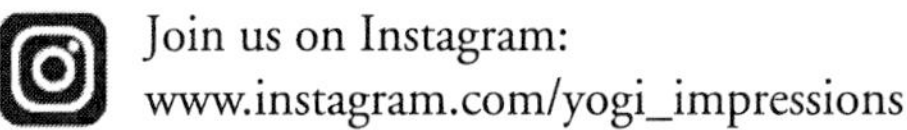
Join us on Instagram:
www.instagram.com/yogi_impressions

ALSO PUBLISHED BY YOGI IMPRESSIONS

The Sacred India Tarot

Inspired by Indian Mythology and Epics

78 cards + 4 bonus cards + 350 page handbook

The Sacred India Tarot is truly an offering from India to the world. It is the first and only Tarot deck that works solely within the parameters of sacred Indian mythology – almost the world's only living mythology today.

ADVAITA
ON
ZEN AND TAO

INSIGHTS ON HUANG PO & LAO TZU
BY RAMESH BALSEKAR

Edited by
Gary Roba and Gautam Sachdeva

YogiImpressions®

ADVAITA ON ZEN AND TAO

First published in India in 2008 by

Yogi Impressions LLP

1711, Centre 1, World Trade Centre,

Cuffe Parade, Mumbai 400 005, India.

Website: www.yogiimpressions.com

First Edition, April 2008

Eighth reprint, November 2025

Book design: Priya Mehta

ISBN 978-81-88479-30-6

Printed at: Manipal Technologies Limited